COMEDIES,
THRILLERS, EPICS
MUSICALS,
LOVESTORIES,
WESTERNS,
WAR FILMS
and others
by
JOEL W. FINLER
introduction by
DUSTIN
HOFFMAN

All-Time
MOVIE
FAVORITES

OCTOPUS

CONTENTS

Introduction	8
The Silents	10
Studios and Stars	28
The War and After	62
Independents and Others	90
The Cinema goes Modern	132
New Directions	164
Index and Acknowledgments	186

First published in 1977 by
Octopus Books Limited
59 Grosvenor Street, London W1

© 1975 Hennerwood Publications Limited

ISBN 0 904230 13 9

Produced by Mandarin Publishers Limited
Hong Kong

For Ben and Tillie

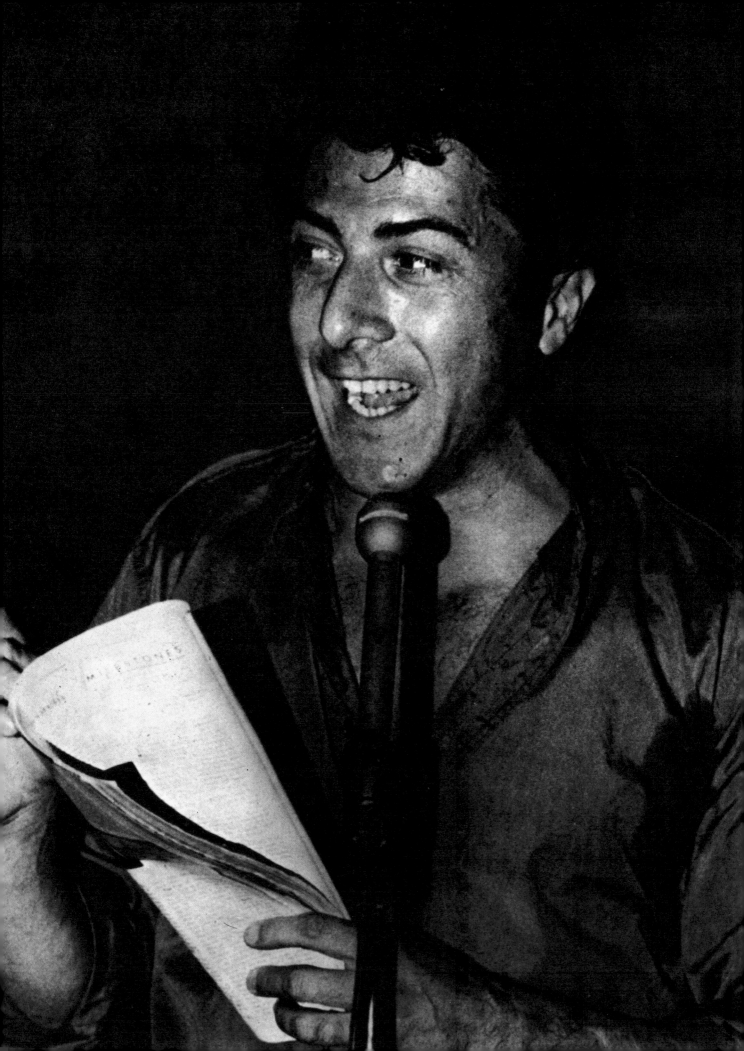

In assembling this book, which is about 200 of the greatest movies to have come from Hollywood and London, with its inevitable emphasis on the work of the directors, the editors felt it would be appropriate also to hear from an actor – to have a personal memoir from a man who is indeed one of the most respected movie actors of our time, Dustin Hoffman.

Notes From In Front Of The Camera

"On reading this book, I was naturally pleased to find that three of my films had been included. In particular, I was even more pleased that the editors had chosen the three that are my favourites too!

"The screen test for *The Graduate* was a disaster. But Mike Nichols saw something in me that he could use. Panic, maybe? It was Nichols' picture – his victory rather than mine. But what an opportunity for a beginner! More recently, *Lenny* is simply the best role I've had since *Ratso* in *Midnight Cowboy*. (Anyone who comes to New York and isn't a millionaire feels as lonely as the Cowboy and Ratso.) People sometimes suggest the two roles are in some way related, but I don't think they are except possibly to me in the purely personal sense that Ratso represents that part of myself that feels inadequate, fraudulent; and Lenny is that part of myself that feels important, unique.

"Not that I even thought of being an actor when I was a kid. I only got the part of Tiny Tim in my school Christmas play because when they lined us all up, I was the shortest. School was like that. I can remember being so self conscious about my nose that if I was talking to a girl in the schoolyard, or at lunch, I made sure that I was talking to her full on. And I'd never walk away in profile.

"I never took an acting course until I was in college and then just as an easy way to earn a credit. Though after the second week in class, I was hooked. Which leads me to another film, and another actor, that I would have been mortified not to find in this book, for if there was one actor who was an inspiration to me, and one performance which was an inspiration to all of us actors "plummeting to stardom" in ramshackle apartments in New York, it was Marlon Brando in *Streetcar Named Desire*.

"When you watch Brando, you see what an actor can be – portraying a character in order to personalize him, to elevate him, to make him a real person. Lee Strasberg always said, "There is no such thing as a leading man. There are no leading men in life. Every person is a character. When you say 'Gee, that guy is like a leading man' he immediately becomes a character".

"I agree with that. Maybe it's one reason why I enjoy playing oddballs, eccentrics, old men, in a word – characters. I remember once saying I wanted to become the world's greatest character lover! (Though maybe that was just a hangover from announcing to the family that I intended to become an actor and having my Aunt respond instantly, "You can't – you're not good looking enough".)

"There are many characters that still intrigue me. Hitler has always been an enigma and a challenge to me. And I would like to do a film on the Hollywood political climate of the 1950's – which has never really been done. Dalton Trumbo would be a great character to centre on. Who knows, maybe if I am lucky, one of them will turn up in some future edition of this book!

"Not that you can ever be sure what people will say about your work. Of course, everybody likes to get good reviews. It's just a stay of execution as far as I am concerned. You still have to look forward to the worst which will come maybe with the next review, when it will finally be revealed to all, including yourself, that you are a fraud.

"But, of course, what matters is your own feeling about the work. You see your own work and you know yourself what's good and what's bad. You know where you could go back and improve it and you wish you could.

"That always exists – and it's never going to stop existing."

New York   *Dustin Hoffman*

CHAPTER 1

THE SILENTS

EARLY CLASSICS

The two most famous names associated with the American cinema during the middle and late teens were D. W. Griffith and Charlie Chaplin, but Edwin S. Porter had first pioneered the story film over ten years earlier.

Although not the first story film or even the first Western, **The Great Train Robbery** (Edison, 1903) is probably the best known picture in the first fifteen years of movies and a landmark in the development of the American cinema.

Directed by Edwin S. Porter, working for the Edison Company, *The Great Train Robbery* was full of action, exciting to watch and topical as well, for the Hole in the Wall gang or Wild Bunch, whose members included Butch Cassidy and the Sundance Kid, were still holding up trains in the Far West.

Inventive composition and the staging of scenes in long shot conceals the absence of editing in the modern sense. In the opening scene, set inside a telegraph office, the train is seen through the window; and the shot of the robbery is actually filmed on the moving roof of the train. There is a memorable final scene, set in a wooded grove, in which the bandits divide up the loot while the posse creep up unobserved from the background before opening fire.

The picture's success helped to establish a foothold for the new medium and also influenced film-makers in Britain where chase pictures such as *Rescued by Rover* (1905) were enormously popular.

It is difficult today to appreciate the impact of D. W. Griffith's **The Birth of a Nation** (Griffith/Epoch, 1914). Although several large-scale, feature-length films had already been made in Europe, notably *Quo Vadis* (1912) and *Cabiria* (1913), Griffith was the first director to exploit the full potential of the new medium. Significant for its exploration of theme and character, the film was also a commercial success. Costing about $100,000 to make, it is estimated to have earned between $20 million and $60 million!

Set during the Civil War period, the film, running for over three hours, encompasses a vast panorama of characters and events, skilfully blending fiction with historical fact. After a brief prologue depicting the introduction of slavery, the first half concentrates on the war, including some dramatic battle sequences, Sherman's march through Georgia and the surrender of Lee; and the second half deals with the postwar reconstruction of the South.

Despite its epic scale, the film preserves the elements of an intimate chronicle, centred on an aristocratic Southern family, complete with a double love story. The

climax is pure Western, with the Ku Klux Klan, no less, riding to the rescue of the 'goodies', besieged by a band of renegade blacks.

Intolerance (Griffith/Wark, 1916), although in many respects a greater artistic achievement than *The Birth of a Nation*, was a box-office failure, largely as a result of the colossal production expenses. Financed from the earlier film's profits, it cost roughly twenty times more – over $2 million. But it hardly had the makings of a popular success and audiences were baffled by Griffith's choice of subject and his technical innovations. The film ran for three and a half hours in its original version, telling four separate stories simultaneously, with regular crosscutting from one to another.

The picture was certainly not lacking in spectacular appeal. In the Babylon episode, with its fantastic 300-foot-high set and impressive battle sequences (for the Fall of Babylon there were 15,000 extras and 250 chariots on call for a single day's filming), Griffith far surpassed the popular Italian costume epics of the time. But film audiences evidently found all this magnificence difficult to equate with the parallel modern story in which Griffith dealt boldly with such contemporary American social themes as strike-breaking, slum life and prison conditions. Furthermore, the pacifist message of the picture did not go down well with a nation gearing itself to enter the European war. Despite these initial disadvantages, however, *Intolerance* later established itself as an undisputed classic.

Douglas Fairbanks

"The Thief of Bagdad"

1924

HISTORICAL BLOCK-BUSTERS

The costume spectacle has always been popular with film audiences; and the two most famous names associated with this type of picture during the Twenties were Cecil B. DeMille and Douglas Fairbanks Sr.

The story of the making of **Ben-Hur** from 1923–25 strikingly resembles that of *Cleopatra* some 40 years later. Film rights alone cost more than half a million dollars. Months were spent testing stars for the title role before George Walsh was selected, while Charles Brabin was chosen to direct instead of the favourite, Rex Ingram. Furthermore, initial filming in Italy was hampered by the unsettled political situation brought about by Mussolini's rise to power.

In 1924 the newly formed M.G.M. took over what had started as a Sam Goldwyn production. All footage shot so far was discarded, Fred Niblo was appointed director and Ramon Novarro got the title role. Cast and crew returned home in 1925. The giant Circus Maximus set, designed for the famous chariot race, was rebuilt in Hollywood and was made to look larger by the use of superb trick photography. The race, one of the most dramatic and exciting sequences ever filmed, was partially copied in the 1959 remake. With certain sequences even shot in two-tone colour. *Ben-Hur* cost about $4 million – the most expensive silent film ever. Yet it grossed more than twice that amount and added immeasurably to the prestige of M.G.M. (See previous page.)

The Ten Commandments (Famous Players-Lasky, 1924) was the first of a group of Biblical/Roman epics made over the years by producer-director Cecil B. DeMille, (seen below with producer Adolf Zukor) later examples being *King of Kings* (1927), *The Sign of the Cross* (1932), *Cleopatra* (1934) and *Samson and Delilah* (1949). This early version of *The Ten Commandments* (which he remade in 1956) incorporates a somewhat melodramatic modern story about two brothers – one good, the other bad – played by Richard Dix and Rod la Roque; but essentially the film relied for its success on sheer spectacle.

In the City of Rameses, the picture boasted what was claimed to be the largest-ever exterior set, exceeding the Babylon of *Intolerance* and the castle in *Robin Hood*. Its construction required 550,000 feet of timber, 300 tons of plaster, 25,000 pounds of nails and 75 miles of cable and wire. And some 33,000 yards (nearly 19 miles) of cloth were used for the costumes!

The most original works of DeMille as a director were his earliest silent films, which included *The Squaw Man* (1913) and *The Cheat* (1915). During 1918–22 he directed pictures that reflected the period's new morality, occasionally turning to comedy, as in his entertaining version of Barrie's *The Admirable Crichton*, retitled *Male and Female* (1920), starring Gloria Swanson. But essentially DeMille remained a showman with a great gift for anticipating and adjusting to the demands of popular taste.

The Thief of Baghdad (Fairbanks/United Artists, 1924), together with *Robin Hood* (1922), marked the highpoint of Douglas Fairbank's transformation from the genial, acrobatic comedy star of the postwar years into the dashing, all-American, swashbuckler hero of such spectacular costume films as *The Mark of Zorro* (1920), *The Three Musketeers* (1921), etc.

A witty, imaginative work, freely adapted from *The Thousand and One Nights*, *The Thief of Bagdad* brings a fairy-tale world to life on the screen – complete with giant urns, fearsome sea monsters, a flying horse, a terrible dragon, a beautiful princess and an invading Mongol army.

Fairbanks's lively style of acting is perfectly matched here by the inspired sets of William Cameron Menzies. But in this and other films during the Twenties Fairbanks not only starred but was producer, scenario writer and supervisor of all stages of film-making. With Charlie Chaplin, D. W. Griffith and his wife, Mary Pickford, he helped found United Artists in 1919.

The Thief of Bagdad and the war film, *What Price Glory?* (1926), were the two outstanding contributions to the silent cinema of director Raoul Walsh, whose Hollywood career spanned almost half a century.

TWENTIES REALISM

A Dog's Life and *Shoulder Arms* were the first pictures made by Chaplin for First National in 1918 when his familiar comic tramp figure was the best loved, most famous movie character in the world. After directing and starring in his own films at the Mack Sennett Keystone studios, he had moved to Essanay and then to Mutual where he produced such classic shorts as *The Vagabond*, *One A.M.*, *The Pawnshop*, *Easy Street*, *The Cure* and *The Immigrant*. In his *Autobiography* Chaplin noted, 'In

the Keystone days the tramp had been freer. His brain was seldom active then – only his instincts, which were concerned with the basic essentials: food, warmth and shelter. But with each succeeding comedy the tramp grew more complex.'

Of *A Dog's Life* he later recalled, 'The story had an element of satire, paralleling the life of a dog with that of a tramp. I was beginning to think of comedy in a structural sense, and to become conscious of its architectural form. The first sequence was rescuing a dog from a fight with other dogs. The next was rescuing a girl in a dance-hall who was also leading "a dog's life". As simple and obvious as these comedies were, a great deal of thought

and invention went into them. If a gag interfered with the logic of events however funny it was, I would not use it.'

Filmed and edited by Robert Flaherty during 1920–2, **Nanook of the North** (Revillon Frères) gained new audience acceptance for the 'non-fiction' type of picture and brought immediate fame and prestige to its creator, now dubbed 'father of the documentary'. Originally an explorer of northern Canada's Hudson Bay area, Flaherty had taken a movie camera on an expedition in 1913. Although his film about Eskimo life was destroyed by fire, he determined to make another. Not only was *Nanook* shot under the most rigorous conditions but Flaherty even developed and printed much of the film as he went along, cutting a hole through eight feet of ice to obtain the water he needed. 'It has always been most important for me to see my rushes,' wrote Flaherty. 'It is the only way I can make a film. But another reason . . . was to project it to the Eskimos so that they would accept and understand what I was doing, and work together with me as partners.' In dramatizing the Eskimo's struggle for survival, Flaherty created an exciting and moving work which has lost none of its power over the years.

During the Twenties Erich von Stroheim established himself as one of the world's most exciting and creative film makers. The fresh, sophisticated treatment of adult subjects in his first pictures reflected the new morality and sexual freedom of the immediate postwar period. **Foolish Wives** (Universal, 1922) marks the high point of his early career as a director. It is a typically cultivated triangle drama, acted out in a Continental setting, and contains Stroheim's own most remarkable film performance.

Greed (Goldwyn/M.G.M., 1924) is the most ambitious and extraordinary film directed by Stroheim during his stormy career. Closely based on the novel McTeague by Frank Norris, and superbly photographed in California and Death Valley, the film's striking visual appearance and larger-than-life qualities go far beyond simple realism, aided by outstanding performances from ZaSu Pitts, Jean Hersholt and Gibson Gowland.

Given a free hand by producer Sam Goldwyn, Stroheim ended up with a film lasting about nine hours. He reduced it by roughly one half, envisaging that it would be shown in two parts, but the picture was eventually cut for release in one three-hour entity. Even in this mutilated form, however, it remains one of the greatest achievements of the silent cinema.

Stroheim's later silent films included an adaptation of *The Merry Widow* (1926), starring John Gilbert, which bore his own personal stamp, yet proved to be a tremendous popular success; *The Wedding March* (1927); and *Queen Kelly* (1928), starring Gloria Swanson. Although his directorial career was concentrated into the Twenties, Stroheim continued acting in films until his death in 1957. Shortly after World War One, he specialized in portraying villainous German officers, becoming widely known as 'The Man You Love to Hate'. The mythical Stroheim image was reinforced by fictitious biographical details and elaborate publicity stories, making it difficult later for him to find work as a director.

One of the best known, most successful Westerns of the silent period, **The Iron Horse** (Fox, 1924), which made the name of director John Ford, began as a relatively small picture. According to Ford, 'We had to spend more and more money and eventually this simple little story came out as a so-called "epic", the biggest picture that Fox had ever made.'

In dramatizing the race between the Union Pacific and Central Pacific to build the first transcontinental railroad, Ford included a wide range of standard Western themes – the wild frontier town with its fighting, drinking, gambling and loose women, the Pony Express, attacks by Indians, and the cattle drive from Kansas to feed the railroad workers. The tall hero (played by George O'Brien) is matched against a rich, villainous landowner and a

'renegade' Indian leader. Real-life characters such as
Buffalo Bill and Wild Bill Hickok put in an appearance,
and the Indian leaders are played by genuine Indians.
Yet despite the scope of the picture, the intimate qualities
of the story are well integrated with the larger historical
events. John Ford is seen above directing.

Sunrise (Fox, 1927) was the brainchild and creation of
two leading talents of the German cinema – script-
writer Carl Mayer and director Friedrich Murnau – but
was filmed in Hollywood with an American cast. The
pair's previous film, *The Last Laugh*, had been a great
success in the U.S. and Murnau was virtually given a
free hand. As Lotte Eisner noted, 'All the skill Murnau
had developed in Germany in the years from 1919 to
1926 are here made manifest in the most dazzling manner:
his marvellous sense of camera, lighting and tone values,
his mastery of the composition and rhythmic ordering
of images. And his gift for creating atmosphere.'

The story tells of a young farmer (George O'Brien),
torn between love for his wife (Janet Gaynor) and attrac-
tion to a sophisticated lady from the city. At the first
Academy Award ceremony the film won an Oscar for
'artistic quality of production', while the cameramen and
Janet Gaynor also won Oscars. Murnau's later films in
the U.S. included *The Four Devils* (1928), *Our Daily
Bread* (1930) and his remarkable last picture *Tabu* (1931),
in collaboration with Robert Flaherty.

CLASSIC COMEDY

Silent film comedy reached its high point in the mid-Twenties, with notable contributions from the famous foursome – Chaplin, Keaton, Langdon and Lloyd. All had begun their film careers by starring in one- and two-reel comedies and had later graduated to features.

After his remarkable first feature, *The Kid* (1920), Chaplin returned to making shorts, and then directed a serious comedy of manners, *The Woman of Paris* (1923), which, although now forgotten, influenced directors such as Ernst Lubitsch, who made *The Marriage Circle* in the following year. In **The Gold Rush** (United Artists, 1925) Chaplin established the pattern of carefully planned and executed feature-length films, which he both directed and starred in, at regular intervals over the next 30 years.

In *The Gold Rush* the familiar tramp appears, for the only time, far from his native setting – a small, dark figure, carrying a pack as well as the customary cane, silhouetted against a vast expanse of snow. He edges his way along a narrow ledge, unaware of a huge bear close behind, eventually reaching a cabin where he meets gold prospector Big Jim (Mack Swain). Isolated by the blizzard, Charlie cooks and eats his boot, while Big Jim, delirious from the lack of food, keeps imagining Charlie transformed into a plump chicken and gives chase.

The pace slackens a bit in the second half but all ends happily as the friends strike it rich and Charlie gets his girl.

Buster Keaton graduated from shorts to features in the early Twenties, and **The General** (Keaton/Schenck/ United Artists, 1926) marked the high-spot of his career as writer-director and star of his own pictures. Beautifully designed and photographed, the films transcend mere slapstick and rank today as more complete works of art than those of Chaplin. Although most of them have contemporary settings, Keaton could handle period subjects too. A Northerner himself, he had a special affection for the South of a century or more ago. In *Our Hospitality* (1923) he mingled Southern hospitality with Southern feuding to produce high comedy. The Mississippi steamboats provide the setting for *Steamboat Bill Jr* (1928); and *The General* is based on a true Civil War incident when Northern spies tried to steal a locomotive and sabotage Southern rail lines.

The film develops into an extended railway chase, providing Keaton with the chance for some remarkable stunt work, brilliant comic characterization (as a determined little engineer who refuses to surrender his favourite locomotive, no matter how impossible the odds against him) and superb location photography, including highly convincing battle scenes.

When the domination of the big studios during the early Thirties deprived Keaton of his creative independence, the world lost both a great comic and a great film-maker.

Safety Last (Hal Roach/Pathé, 1923) was the best known of Harold Lloyd's feature films, containing the memorable sequence of him climbing a skyscraper like a human fly and coming up against the most unexpected and hair-raising obstacles. Filmed without double exposure or trick photography, according to Lloyd himself, 'the illusion lay in deceptive camera angles of drop and height.' Occupying almost one-third of the film, this sequence provides a breathtaking climax and serves as the logical outcome of the aspirations of Harold, the bespectacled boy-next-door, determined to succeed in life against overwhelming odds. This quality of cheerful perseverance and pluck endeared Lloyd to film audiences throughout the Twenties when he became one of Hollywood's most successful (and richest) stars.

Harry Langdon's best known films are concentrated into four years – 1924–5, as a Mack Sennett star in numerous shorts, and 1926–7, when he made three memorable features with writer-director Frank Capra – *Long Pants*, *The Strong Man* and *Tramp, Tramp, Tramp*, with Joan Crawford in an early role.

In **The Strong Man** (Langdon/First National, 1926), after fighting off the enemy on a World War One battlefield with a slingshot and ration biscuits, Langdon is captured by a giant German who trails him along as a kind of mascot when he later tours the U.S. as a strong man. A hilarious series of escapades leads to the climax when, as stand-in for the strong man, Langdon destroys the town saloon – local den of iniquity – and wins his girl.

In all his films Langdon shows a remarkable naïveté and innocence – a grown-up man with the face and mind of a child, lost in a strange, baffling world. He is unaffected by the most extraordinary adventures, the significance of which he cannot understand. With his subtle gestures and facial expressions he is, as James Agee noted, 'a virtuoso of hesitations and of delicately indecisive motions.'

WAR FILMS

Pictures about the Great War were not popular in the U.S. during the early Twenties. *Hearts of the World* and *Shoulder Arms*, both filmed in 1918, had the prestige, respectively, of D. W. Griffith and Chaplin. But between 1918 and 1925 the only war film of note was *The Four Horsemen of the Apocalypse*, which launched a new star – Valentino.

The Big Parade (M.G.M. 1925) was originally designed as a star vehicle for John Gilbert. Directed by King Vidor and produced by Irving Thalberg, the film was conceived as a serious treatment of the war theme, in the tradition of *The Birth of a Nation*.

The battle scenes remain outstanding and foreshadow similar sequences in *All Quiet on the Western Front* five years later (as in the hero's encounter with an enemy soldier whom he is unable to kill and to whom he offers a cigarette). The 'big parade' itself is a seemingly endless line of troops and trucks, with planes overhead, all heading into battle, and filmed in a remarkable single shot.

Vidor continued to make films of a consistently high standard for more than 30 years. Adapting easily to the coming of sound, he completed one of the finest late silent pictures, *The Crowd*, in 1928, following this with an all-Negro sound musical, *Hallelujah!* (1929), which retains its power and vitality even today. Later memorable Vidor films included *Our Daily Bread* (1934), *Duel in the Sun* (1946) and *War and Peace* (1956).

Based on a popular novel by Ibáñez, **The Four Horsemen of the Apocalypse** (Metro, 1921) concerns a Spanish family in the Argentine and the manner in which the younger generation get caught up on opposing sides of the war in Europe. The plot is rather fragmented and sprawling, and the attitude to war a little naïve, but the picture is stylishly directed by Irish-born Rex Ingram and visually striking (photographed by his regular cameraman, John Seitz). And there is Rudolph Valentino as the 'good' son who goes off to war, transformed from a cigarette-smoking, tango-dancing playboy into a seasoned soldier.

The film turned Valentino into a star, made the name of Rex Ingram, who later made romantic films such as *The Prisoner of Zenda* (1922) and *Scaramouche* (1923), both starring Ramon Novarro, and rescued its studio, Metro, from financial straits.

Wings (Paramount/Famous Players-Lasky, 1927) was the first of a group of major pictures based on the exploits of the fliers of World War One. Others filmed during the late silent and early sound period included *Hell's Angels* (1930), *The Dawn Patrol* (1930) and *The Last Flight* (1931). Directed by William Wellman, himself a former pilot, *Wings* was the first picture, and the only silent, to win an Oscar. It traces the experiences of two cadets from their first enlistment and training through the grim realities of war. Gary Cooper makes a brief but memorable appearance as a fatalistic flier who leaves the two recruits with their first taste of death; and Clara Bow is superb as the lively girl-next-door who later turns up driving an ambulance truck in France.

The silent, beautiful world above the clouds is stunningly evoked, its peace soon shattered by the appearance of enemy planes and the onset of battle. As Julian Fox has noted, 'Wellman and his fifteen cameramen invested the aerial scenes with a dazzling combination of poetic image and breathtaking excitement. Like malevolent gnats, the tiny planes circle and swoop, weave and dive through startling cloud formations or over deserted countryside.' With its amazing sequences of stunt flying and its remarkably convincing ground battle scenes (shot on location in Texas) *Wings* is truly a motion picture to remember.

EARLY SOUND FILMS

In 1926 Warner Bros, in financial trouble, took a gamble by introducing a continuous soundtrack into *Don Juan*, starring John Barrymore. Its success led to *The Jazz Singer*, a limited talkie with some synchronized song and dialogue. Premiered in October 1927, it marked the effective beginning of the sound era. Early triumphs in the new medium included Rouben Mamoulian's *Applause*, the Marx Brothers' first film, *Cocoanuts*, and Lubitsch's *The Love Parade*; and of special interest were two films made outside the U.S. – *The Blue Angel* and *Blackmail*.

Josef von Sternberg's **The Blue Angel** (Pommer/UFA, 1929), shot simultaneously in English and German language versions, depicts the gradual decline of a priggish schoolmaster infatuated with a cheap night-club singer. He gives up his job to marry her, under-going various humiliations which lead to his death.

Emil Jannings effectively characterizes 'Professor' Rath, in a performance closely resembling his roles in the German films *Variety* and *The Last Laugh*; but *The Blue Angel* is best remembered for Marlene Dietrich. Discovered by von Sternberg, she is superb in a manner which contrasts radically with her later sophisticated image. The rough earthiness and uncouth appearance of her Lola Lola are perfectly suited to the atmosphere of the sleazy club where most of the action takes place. The film was shot entirely in the studio, using Expressionistic

street sets reminiscent of countless German pictures from *The Golem* to *Joyless Street*.

It is appropriate that **Blackmail** (Maxwell/British International, 1929), the first British sound film, should have been directed by Alfred Hitchcock. Already established as one of the leading lights of the silent cinema with such films as *The Lodger* (1926), *The Ring* (1927) and *The Farmer's Wife* (1928), he now emerged as Britain's most outstanding director, a position he retained throughout the Thirties until his departure for the U.S. in 1939.

The film is one of the landmarks of British cinema. The introduction of sound opened up new avenues for Hitchcock, which he was quick to recognize and exploit. *Blackmail* is notable for its imaginative use of 'subjective' sound to establish the mood of a sequence or penetrate a character's state of mind. For example, an echo effect is used to isolate the word 'knife' in a piece of casual conversation – reflecting the suppressed hysteria of the heroine, implicated the previous night in a knife murder. As usual with Hitchcock, the film works on many levels – as an entertaining suspense-thriller, as a subtle exploration of the complex relationships between innocent and guilty, attacker and victim, police and suspect, and as a technical tour-de-force. The film's dramatic climax takes place at the British Museum including the use of miniatures and trick shots as the villain is pursued by the police and finally falls to his death.

The leading role, played by German-speaking Anny Ondra (below), was ingeniously 'dubbed' by placing behind the camera an English actress who spoke into a microphone, matching the lip movements of the heroine on screen.

CHAPTER 2

STUDIOS AND STARS

THE MAJOR STUDIOS

The Thirties, which began with the Depression and ended with the outbreak of World War Two, were dominated by the studios, especially in the U.S. where all major stars, writers, directors and even bit-players were under contract. And because of the technical demands of sound recording, most of the filming took place on the studio lot or within the four walls of the studio sound stages.

Each studio developed its own style – MGM with lavish, star-studded prestige pictures; Warner Bros with gangster films, Busby Berkeley musicals and Errol Flynn costume pictures; Paramount with romances and the Sternberg/Dietrich films. Columbia was the home of Frank Capra, and Universal was most closely identified with the horror film genre, although its first great success of the Thirties was a picture which powerfully captured on film the profounder horrors of World War One.

One of the most realistic war films ever made, **All Quiet on the Western Front** (Universal, 1930) retains many of the best qualities of the original novel by Erich Maria Remarque, notably in its treatment of the squalor and claustrophobia of life in the trenches and the terrors of hand-to-hand fighting, and in its condemnation of the futile pattern of attack and counter-attack, with the appalling casualties involved. The picture is visually impressive – as when the camera tracks along the trenches and cranes up at one point to observe the advancing troops, or when it pans across the battlefield, littered with corpses. Also remarkable for its time is the down-beat ending, with the death of the young German soldier (Lew Ayres) from a sniper's bullet. Both the film and its director, Lewis Milestone (who made a number of other war movies) were awarded Oscars.

Forty-Second Street (Warners, 1932) was the first example of the 'puttin' on a show' story which has since served as model for countless movies, such as *Cover Girl* (1944), *The Band Wagon* (1953) and, more recently, Ken Russell's *The Boy Friend* (1971). Ruby Keeler enacts the familiar role of unknown chorus girl replacing the star on opening night to save the show, Warner Baxter (right) is the harried, chain-smoking director, and Ginger Rogers plays the gold-digging 'Any-time Annie'. The real star, however, is dance director Busby Berkeley,

responsible for inventive numbers such as 'Shuffle Off To Buffalo', in which the railroad-car set opens out to give a cutaway view of passengers and sleeping berths, and 'I'm Young And Healthy', with complex patterns of circling chorines and fluid camera movements. Other successful Berkeley musicals filmed at Warners during 1933–4 included *Gold Diggers of 1933*, *Footlight Parade* and *Dames*.

The career of Rouben Mamoulian during the early Thirties epitomizes the contrast between Warners and Paramount. His sophisticated, Lubitsch-style musical, **Love Me Tonight** (1932) is as different from the lavish Busby Berkeley spectaculars as his stylish thriller *City Streets* (1931), starring Gary Cooper and Sylvia Sydney, is from the tough, realistic Warners' gangster movies. *Love Me Tonight* blends a witty script with a delightful selection of songs by Rodgers and Hart, reflecting a visual flair and pacing which Mamoulian carried over from his non-musical pictures. Conventions were ignored by having actors such as C. Aubrey Smith sing with their own, unpolished voices, yet a fine sense of rhythm and movement was preserved. The famous number 'Isn't it Romantic?' for example, develops from a conversation between a tailor (Maurice Chevalier) and his customer, is

31

picked up by a taxi-driver, and is carried along by a composer-passenger, a troop of soldiers and a gypsy fiddler, before finally being overheard by the princess-heroine (Jeanette MacDonald). Naturally the tailor-hero eventually meets, woos and wins his princess.

Dr Jekyll and Mr Hyde, the well-known story by Robert Louis Stevenson, has been adapted to the screen several times – with John Barrymore in 1920, with Spencer Tracy in 1941, and in the Jean Renoir/Jean-Louis Barrault version of 1959. The 1931 adaptation provided a further example of Mamoulian's diversity as a director at Paramount during this period and brought Fredric March an Oscar for his performance in the famous dual role. March portrays both Jekyll and Hyde as fully developed characters, contrasted not only in appearance and behaviour but also in gestures and movements. In one extraordinary chase sequence near the end of the film, Hyde swings adroitly down the banisters, revealing his true ape-man personality.

The addition of two contrasting female characters (Miriam Hopkins being excellent as the 'bad girl' who comes to a sticky end) underlines the emotional conflicts of Jekyll/Hyde. The transformation scene is justly famous, the atmosphere of Victorian London is admirably recreated, and the film is also notable for the explicitness of its eroticism.

Public Enemy (1931), directed by William Wellman, of *Wings* fame, is one of the two best known of Warners' gangster films in the early Thirties, the other being *Little Caesar* (1930). The latter film made the name of Edward G. Robinson, and in *Public Enemy* James Cagney, best known as a song and dance man, achieved stardom almost by accident. After only three days of shooting, Wellman switched his leading actors, giving Cagney the part of the 'public enemy' and Eddie Woods that of his sidekick.

The film traces the rapid rise and fall of a pair of gangsters during the early Prohibition era. Cagney first makes his mark by 'selling' his beer to reluctant bartenders and demonstrates his ruthless style by planting a grapefruit in Mae Clarke's face; but it is Jean Harlow who is featured as the most memorable of his successive blonde girl friends. In one of the film's nicely unexpected touches, the unarmed Cagney, on the run from a rival gang, enters a gun shop, innocently asks for a weapon and is patiently instructed in loading and aiming. He then turns the gun on the astonished owner of the shop, barking, 'This is a stick-up!'

The PUBLIC ENEMY

JAMES CAGNEY · JEAN HARLOW
EDWARD WOODS · JOAN BLONDELL

STORY BY KUBEC GLASMON and JOHN BRIGHT
SCREEN ADAPTATION by HARVEY THEW

Directed by WILLIAM A. WELLMAN

A WARNER BROS.
and VITAPHONE
Production

In **Shanghai Express** (Paramount, 1932) director Josef von Sternberg and his star Marlene Dietrich achieved their greatest popular success of the period. This ingenious blend of fantasy and reality received an Oscar for best photography (by Lee Garmes, who had worked with the same director and star on *Morocco* and *Dishonoured*) and a nomination as best film of the year.

The picture describes the adventures of a trainload of passengers travelling from Peking to Shanghai, the highlight being a raid by Chinese revolutionaries led by a ruthless Warner Oland; but it is essentially a vehicle for Dietrich, superb as the seductive, scheming 'Shanghai Lily'. As in other Sternberg films of the time (*The Devil is a Woman* (1935) being a notable example), she is so glamorous as to be virtually unattainable, and the ill-treatment dealt out to her various unworthy suitors seems well merited.

At the height of his career during 1928–35, Sternberg directed fourteen feature films, seven of them starring Dietrich; but as a result of ill health and difficulties with producers, his only later films of note were *The Shanghai Gesture* (1941) and *Anatahan* (1953).

Although Mae West had been an established success on Broadway for many years when she arrived in Hollywood, her first big film role, in **She Done Him Wrong** (1933), based on one of her greatest stage hits, *Diamond Lil*, turned her into a star overnight and saved Paramount from bankruptcy. It was also instrumental in forming the Legion of Decency in 1934, leading to a tightening up of film censorship.

A truly original comedienne, Mae West wrote her own stories, scripts and memorable lines of dialogue, such as, 'It's not the men in my life, but the life in my men . . .', full of witty sexual innuendos and double meanings. Her characteristically slow and meaningful delivery, each syllable stressed for maximum effect, was developed in the theatre and even more outrageously exploited on the screen. 'One of the finest women that ever walked the streets' someone remarks as she makes her first appearance in *She Done Him Wrong*. The story, including counterfeiting, white slave traffic and murder, moves along at a cracking pace. Eventually Mae gets her man – none other than a youthful Cary Grant (below).

Mae West continued to play variations on the same larger-than-life character in such films as *I'm No Angel* (1933), *Belle of the Nineties* (1934), *Go West Young Man* (1936) and *Klondike* (1936).

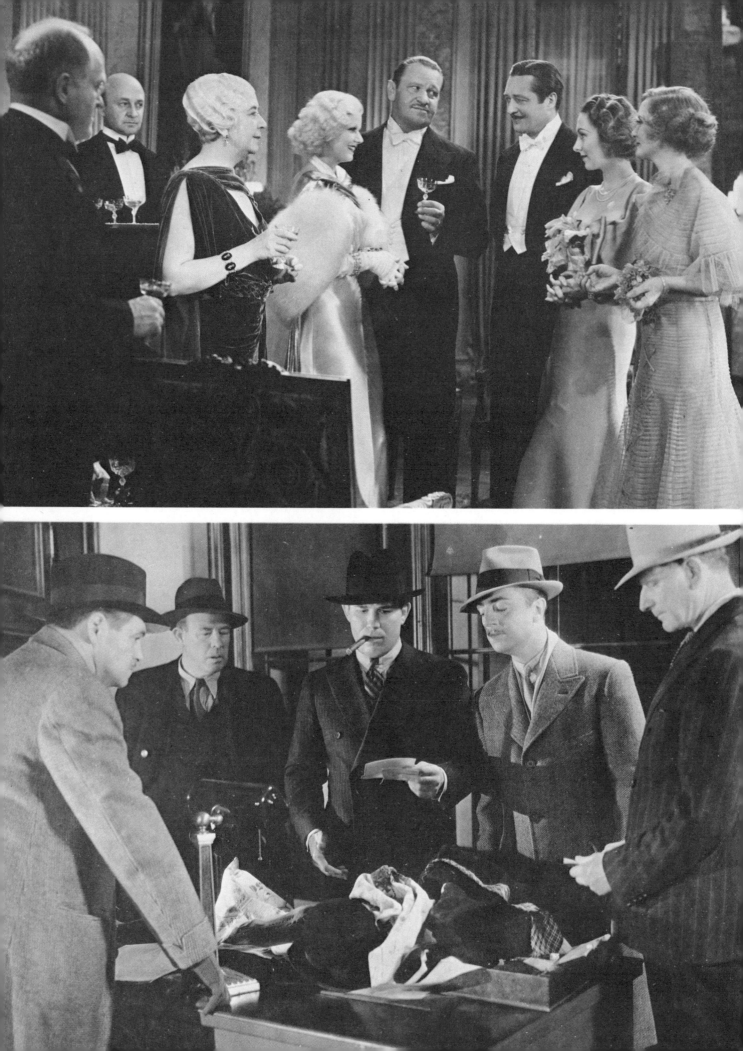

Dinner at Eight (1933), like *Grand Hotel* the previous year, is a prime example of the M.G.M. prestige movie of the period. With several sub-plots, designed partly to show off the talents of the studio's many stars, both films were based on stage plays and had common features. John Barrymore is typically cast in both pictures as the sensitive elderly gentleman at the end of his tether and Wallace Beery as the wheeler-dealer businessman; and there is the young, attractive girl – Jean Harlow (in *Dinner at Eight*) and Joan Crawford (in *Grand Hotel*) – whose kindness to a sympathetic older man (Lionel Barrymore) facing a crisis provides a sort of happy ending, counter-balancing the tragic death of brother John. The elegantly designed sets of Cedric Gibbons and the stylish photography of William Daniels ensure that both films are stunning to look at; and the acting too is generally excellent, reflecting the hand of director George Cukor.

The Thin Man (1934) was the first and best known of the series of sophisticated, witty private-eye pictures which starred William Powell as detective Nick Charles, Myrna Loy as his wife, and their dog Asta. Produced at M.G.M. and directed by W. S. Van Dyke, these movies provide another example of the well-made escapist film which was so popular during the Thirties.

In general, the films follow an entertaining, if predictable, pattern – a murder in mysterious circumstances which baffles the police and brings in Nick to practise a bit of amateur sleuthing, aided, perhaps inadvertently, by wife and dog. In a final grand gesture, he brings all the characters together in one room to reveal the villain – usually the least likely suspect. The explanation may not always be convincing but the result is entertaining.

The success of *The Thin Man* boosted the careers both of male star and director. In 1936 Powell appeared in two memorable film roles – *My Man Godfrey* and *The Great Ziegfeld*; and Van Dyke was assigned to direct the prestige picture *San Francisco*.

A rare example in the cinema of a sequel improving on an original, **The Bride of Frankenstein** (Universal, 1935), like *Frankenstein* before it, was directed by English-born James Whale, who had arrived in Hollywood in 1929 to direct the film version of R. C. Sherriff's *Journey's End*, after designing and producing this play in London.

The Bride of Frankenstein had a largely British cast which included Elsa Lanchester, Valerie Hobson, Ernest Thesiger (as a delightfully wicked mad scientist) and, of course, Boris Karloff as the monster. The film enabled Whale to indulge his taste for black humour and witty dialogue. Especially memorable is Thesiger's first visit to the crypt and meeting with the monster: 'I rather like this place; I think I'll stay for a while.' The monster itself is sympathetically portrayed – laughing, talking and even enjoying a cigar – which gives added poignancy to the unexpected climax when he is rejected by his new mate. The first appearance of the monster-bride is heightened, as noted by Carlos Clarens, '. . . by a riotous display of unusual camera angles, fast editing and electrical effects . . . Elsa Lanchester, in her white shroud and Nefertiti hairdo, is a truly fantastic apparition. With Karloff she manages to communicate a delicate suggestion of both the wedding bed and the grave.'

EARLY THIRTIES BRITISH

During the early Thirties two of the best known and most successful British films were directed by men whose influence in the role of both producer and director was to span more than two decades – Alexander Korda and Victor Saville.

As the most famous British picture of its day, **The Private Life of Henry VIII** (Korda/London Films, 1933) proved a great triumph for producer-director Alexander Korda and for Charles Laughton, giving one of the most memorable screen performances ever. Korda and his predominantly European team of collaborators were not too concerned with historical accuracy, aiming to present an unconventional, earthy image of life at the Tudor court, highlighting the king's relationship with his succession of wives and mistresses. The result was instant success for all concerned. Exploiting the talents of an all-British cast, the movie established Laughton as a star of the first rank (he won an Oscar) and made the names of Robert Donat, Merle Oberon (Korda's future wife) and Elsa Lanchester (Laughton's wife).

The film, shot on a relatively modest budget, proved that it was possible for a British picture to be a major international success. But attempts by Korda and other English producers to repeat the triumph by aping the vast-scale production methods of Hollywood studios were largely unfulfilled. Korda and Laughton collaborated again on *Rembrandt* (1936) but the film, though excellent, did not achieve the same popularity.

Evergreen (Gaumont-British 1934) was the best known of an entertaining series of musicals starring Jessie Matthews and directed by Victor Saville during the mid-Thirties, which also included *The Good Companions* (1932), adapted from J. B. Priestley's novel, *First a Girl* (1935) and *It's Love Again* (1936). Typically British in flavour, these films substituted charm and wit for the lavish spectacle and technical expertise identified with the American musicals of the period. But unfortunately they were overshadowed by the appearance, at the same time, of the first Astaire–Rogers pictures.

Evergreen tells the story of a music-hall star at the turn of the century who has had an illegitimate daughter and is blackmailed into premature retirement. The daughter eventually turns up as a remarkably talented facsimile of her famous mother, thus providing a dual role for Miss Matthews (below right). The direction had the characteristic lightness of touch of Victor Saville. A much underrated talent, his long list of credits included social dramas such as *South Riding* (1937) and *The Citadel* (1938), and spy thrillers like *I was a Spy* (1933), *Kim* (1950), and one of the first Mickey Spillane pictures, *The Long Wait* (1954), starring Anthony Quinn.

THE SMALL STUDIOS

The big Hollywood studios did not make all the running. A surprisingly large proportion of the most successful pictures of the period came from smaller studios such as Columbia or R.K.O., or from independent producers such as David O. Selznick, Howard Hughes and Walter Wanger.

Produced by Howard Hughes and directed by Howard Hawks, **Scarface** (United Artists, 1932) brought to a close that first cycle of American gangster films begun by Sternberg's *Underworld* five years earlier. *Scarface* is a thinly disguised version of the rise to power of Al Capone (here called Tony Camonte and played superbly by Paul

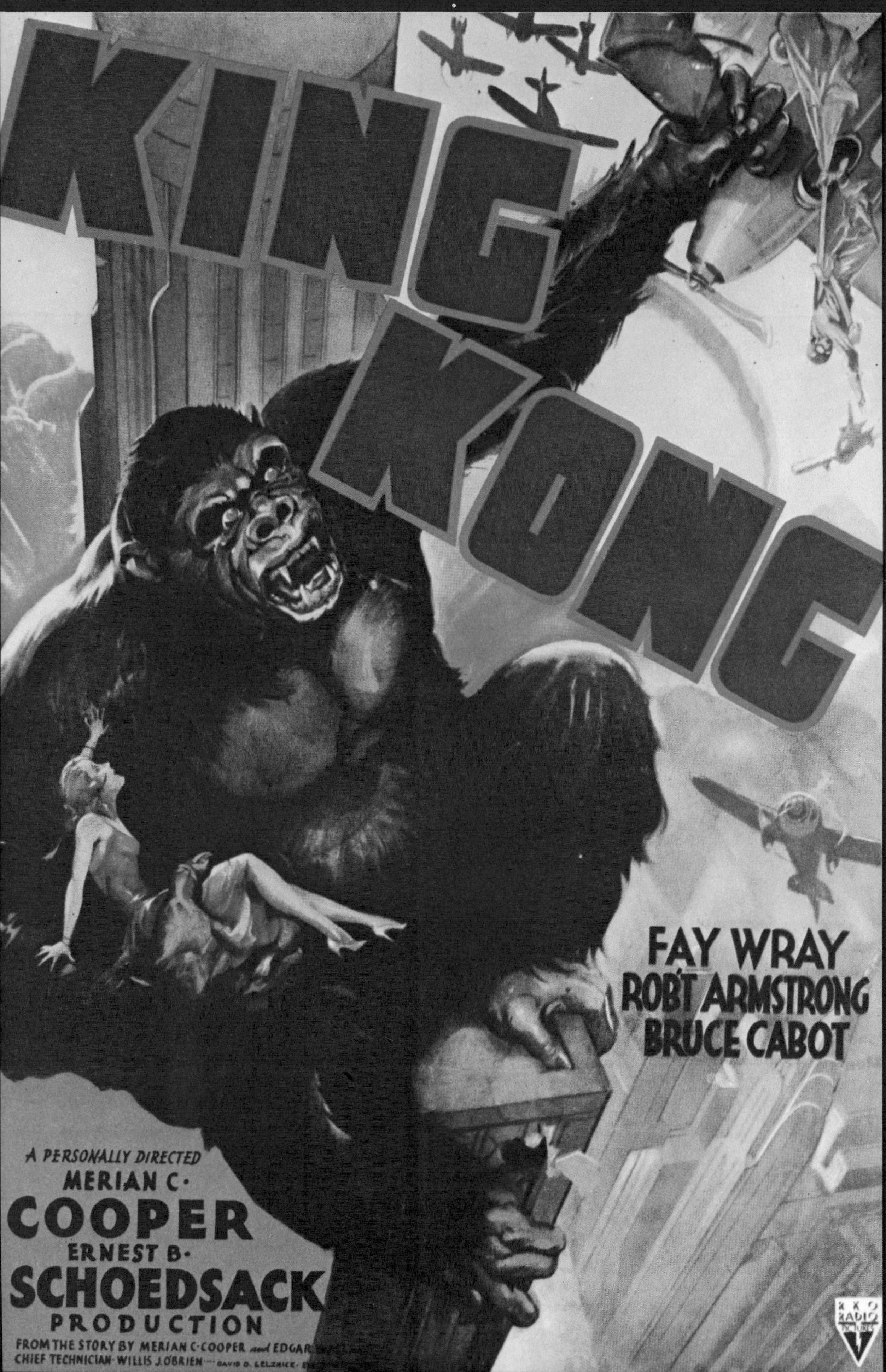
KING KONG
FAY WRAY
ROB'T ARMSTRONG
BRUCE CABOT
A PERSONALLY DIRECTED
MERIAN C. COOPER
ERNEST B. SCHOEDSACK
PRODUCTION
FROM THE STORY BY MERIAN C. COOPER and EDGAR
CHIEF TECHNICIAN WILLIS J. O'BRIEN
DAVID O. SELZNICK

Muni), and is largely based on true incidents such as the St Valentine's Day Massacre of 1929. Direction and editing are fast-paced and the film does not dwell on violence, the frequent killings being treated in an understated manner.

Just as the gangster films of the early Thirties established Robinson and Cagney as stars, so *Scarface* made the names of George Raft and Paul Muni. The latter gives remarkable depth to the character of Camonte, whose rapid climb to power is accomplished by the simple solution of killing anyone who gets in his way. Full of energy, he resembles an overgrown child delighting in showing off his new acquisitions – fancy clothes and bullet-proof car – which come with gang-leader status. But his fall is as swift as his rise, and he dies beneath a Cook's Tours sign flashing the ironic message, 'The World is Yours'.

King Kong (1933) is the most remarkable and durable of adventure-fantasy movies, retaining a certain primitive charm and much of its impact even today. A talented team at R.K.O. included writer Edgar Wallace, composer Max Steiner, directors Merian C. Cooper and Ernest Schoedsack, and special-effects expert Willis O'Brien who had perfected a stop-motion method for animating life-size models of prehistoric animals.

The story tells of a documentary film-maker who, with a view to introducing some 'sex-appeal' into his next picture, offers the job to a young girl down on her luck. Fay Wray, the archetypal horror-film heroine cast for this role, recalled that Cooper told her '. . . I was going to have the tallest, darkest leading man in Hollywood. Naturally, I thought of Clark Gable.' She got a giant gorilla instead. On a Polynesian island inhabited by prehistoric monsters the film makers discover Kong, who rules supreme until fatally attracted to Fay. Captured, brought back to New York and exhibited as the 'Eighth Wonder of the World', he breaks loose and wreaks havoc in the city. Finally the enormous ape climbs to the top of the Empire State Building, where he is attacked and killed by a squadron of fighter planes.

It Happened One Night (1934) is the best-known example of a relatively small-budget, small-studio success in the Thirties. Columbia initially offered the leading roles to Robert Montgomery and Myrna Loy, who declined. Clark Gable and Claudette Colbert were at first equally unenthusiastic but their attitudes changed during shooting, when everyone realized that the picture was going to be something special.

A runaway heiress (Colbert) is promised help by a newspaper reporter (Gable) to find her fiancée in New York. He secretly writes up the story as a scoop, they fall in love, are separated through a misunderstanding, but are happily united at the end. Colbert presents an appealing blend of fragility and resourcefulness, while Gable displays a hitherto neglected talent for comedy. He was loaned to Columbia by M.G.M.

The movie won all five major Oscars – best film, actor, actress, director and screenplay – and was Columbia's first major success. Credit was mainly due to director Frank Capra who was to develop the same mixture of comedy and small-town Americana in subsequent years with such hits as *Mr Deeds Goes to Town* (1936), *You Can't Take it With You* (1938) and *Mr Smith Goes to Washington* (1939).

THEY'RE DANCING CHEEK-TO-CHEEK AGAIN!

FRED
ASTAIRE

GINGER
ROGERS

TOP
HAT

MUSIC AND LYRICS BY

IRVING
BERLIN

with
EDWARD EVERETT HORTON
HELEN BRODERICK
ERIK RHODES · ERIC BLORE

Directed by MARK SANDRICH
A PANDRO S. BERMAN Production

First paired in supporting roles in *Flying Down to Rio* (1933) at R.K.O., Fred Astaire and Ginger Rogers rocketed to stardom in *The Gay Divorcee* (1934) and **Top Hat** (1935), two pictures with much in common. Both were nominated for Oscars as the best films of their respective years and were produced by the same studio team, including dance director Hermes Pan, designer Van Nest Polglase and director Mark Sandrich. Set in London, Brighton and Venice, both belonged to that familiar musical genre of Americans abroad, such as *Funny Face*, *An American in Paris*, etc.

Top Hat is the more fanciful and lavish, benefiting from an Irving Berlin score and a fine supporting cast, including Edward Everett Horton, Helen Broderick and Eric Blore. The farce-like plot, full of unexpected twists and characters in disguise is not meant to be taken too seriously; but the music and dancing are marvellous. The numbers are neatly integrated into the story line, often occurring in open-air settings and reflecting the moods or feelings of the characters (an innovation of the Astaire–Rogers movies) rather than being confined to elaborate stage sets. In keeping with this approach, the dancing of the famous team always appears natural and spontaneous, yet with a timeless classical quality which is the hallmark of all their musicals.

Although John Ford was leading director at Fox during the Thirties, many of his biggest successes were made for other studios, such as *The Whole Town's Talking* (Columbia, 1935), an unusual, semi-humorous gangster film with Edward G. Robinson in a dual role, and **The Informer** (R.K.O., 1935).

Based on the Liam O'Flaherty novel, *The Informer* deals with a tragic series of events during the Sinn Fein rebellion in Dublin in 1922, when Gypo (Victor McLaglen) informs on his friend Frankie, hoping to use the reward money for his passage to America. Made on a small budget, Ford said of the producers, 'They wouldn't let me work on the lot – they sent me across the street to a dusty old stage, which was great because I was alone and they didn't bother me. They wouldn't build us any real sets though – the city of Dublin was just painted canvas.' Yet the picture effectively captures the atmosphere of the night streets and the tension of the times.

Oscars were won by McLaglen, Ford, composer Max Steiner and Dudley Nichols (screenplay). Of Irish ancestry himself, although born in the U.S., Ford had a particular fondness for Irish subjects. In 1936 he filmed Sean O'Casey's play *The Plough and the Stars*, and later directed *The Quiet Man* (1952) and *The Rising of the Moon* (1957) in Ireland.

Stagecoach (1939) was John Ford's first sound Western, directed for producer Walter Wanger and United Artists. Based on the story 'Stage to Lordsburg' by Ernest Haycox, this most famous of all Westerns employs the familiar pattern of a miscellaneous group of travellers thrown together for a journey through dangerous territory. It is 1875 and Geronimo is on the loose. The principal theme, concerning the fate of the stagecoach and its occupants, is balanced by the personal story of The Ringo Kid (John Wayne) and the dance hall girl Dallas (Claire Trevor). Both stories have a dramatic climax. The celebrated chase and running battle with the Indians ends with a predictable last-minute rescue by the cavalry; and there is a final showdown between Ringo and three baddies. As in the original short story, we, like Dallas, hear the bark of guns but are kept in suspense: 'There were four swift shots beating furiously along the sultry quiet, and a shout, and afterward a longer and longer silence. She put one hand against the door to steady herself, and knew that those shots marked the end of a man and the end of a hope . . . She was thinking all that when she heard the strike of boots on the street's packed earth; and turned to see him, high and square in the muddy sunlight, coming toward her with his smile.'

The making of pictures itself has been a favourite theme of American movies over the years, and one of the best examples of Hollywood's fascination with its own image was **A Star is Born** (United Artists, 1937). Directed by William Wellman for Selznick International from his own original story (for which he received an Oscar), the picture made interesting use of the new three-tone Technicolor process. Colour was generally chosen during this period for historical films or for Westerns featuring bright costumes and lavish sets; but in *A Star is Born*, which was set in contemporary Hollywood, it was deliberately used in a restrained and realistic manner.

The picture tells the familiar tale of the small-town girl arriving in Hollywood, being discovered working as a waitress and becoming a star overnight. The role was played by Janet Gaynor, attempting a screen comeback after having been a leading star during the late silent and early sound era (she won the first acting Oscar in 1928). Gaynor and her leading man, Fredric March, playing the husband whose decline parallels her rise, both received Oscar nominations. They had a fine supporting cast, including the gravel-voiced Lionel Stander, Andy Devine, Edgar Kennedy and May Robson.

HOLLYWOOD /
...the beckoning El Dorado
...Metropolis of Make Believe
in the California hills...

EXTRA Los Angeles DAILY Dispatch
NORMAN MAINE'S BODY FOUND OFF MALIBU:
EX-STAR PERISHES IN TRAGIC ACCIDENT!

COMEDIES

If the coming of sound cut short the careers of silent film comics like Keaton, Langdon and Lloyd, it heralded the arrival in Hollywood of a new style of comedy, exemplified by the Marx Brothers, Mae West and W. C. Fields. The peak years of early sound comedy came in the middle and late Thirties, with Chaplin and Laurel and Hardy the only survivors from the silents.

In **Modern Times** (United Artists, 1935) Chaplin's tramp makes his last screen appearance. The infrequent occurrence of major Chaplin films – there were five-year intervals between *City Lights* (1930), this film, and *The Great Dictator* (1940) – suggests the careful thought and preparation that went into each of his feature-length pictures.

Since 1916 Chaplin had been exploring ideas for a satire on modern progress, featuring futuristic gadgets such as a feeding machine and a 'radio-electric hat that could register one's thoughts'. In the event, *Modern Times* turned out to be more of a satire on new techniques of mass production, influenced by René Clair's *A Nous la Liberté*. Chaplin retained the feeding machine concept, as he notes, '. . . used as a time-saving device so that the workers could continue during the lunch time. The factory sequence resolves itself in the tramp having a nervous breakdown. After his cure, he gets arrested and meets a *gamine* (Paulette Goddard) who has also been arrested for stealing bread. . . . From then on the theme is about two nondescripts trying to get along in modern times. They are involved in the Depression, strikes, riots and unemployment.'

Although it featured music and sound effects, the fact that the film was essentially a 'silent' limited its appeal and it was not a great box-office success.

A satire on American middle-class aspirations, **A Night at the Opera** (1935) pits the Marx Brothers against opera impresario Sig. Rumann, whose eagerness to acquire European singers suggests to Groucho that he is on to a good thing, though he ends up by signing the wrong tenor. Full of the usual wild comedy sequences – including the unforgettable crowded cabin scene on board ship – the picture rightly builds on our expectations of that final 'night (of disruption) at the opera', in which the Marxes rise magnificently to the occasion.

First arriving at Paramount studios on Long Island in 1929 to shoot their first picture, *Cocoanuts*, the Marx Brothers continued to turn out a hilarious series of comedies for Paramount including *Animal Crackers* (1930), *Monkey Business* (1931) and *Horse Feathers* (1932). Their free-wheeling antics in the mythical republic of Freedonia in *Duck Soup* (1933), under director Leo McCarey, represent the peak of their comic genius at Paramount, being followed by *A Night at the Opera*, the finest of their MGM pictures during the late 30's.

Although each had spent a number of years in silent comedies, Laurel and Hardy only joined forces towards the end of the silent era. They easily adapted to sound but continued making the same type of half-hour shorts, only later concentrating on features.

A Chump at Oxford (Hal Roach, 1939) was their last outstanding picture. At the opening they are out of

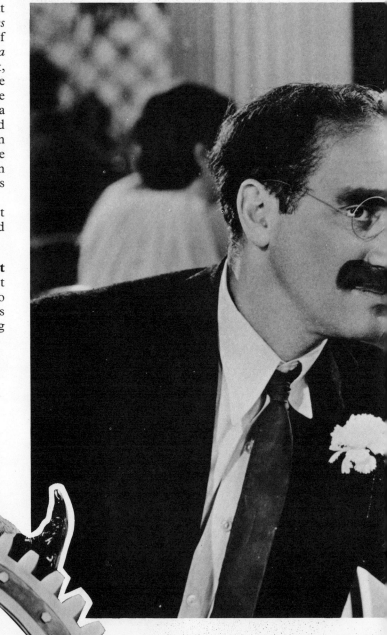

work and take on a variety of jobs which recall earlier shorts. As a maid and butler team, with Stan in 'drag', they disrupt the dinner party thrown by an exasperated James Finlayson. Although British-born Stan was the real creative talent behind their films, on screen he played the eternal simpleton. Here he follows instructions to serve the salad 'without dressing' so literally that the pair are chased off by the host with his shotgun.

At Oxford, where they are sent to be educated, much of the humour revolves around a dual identity situation. Stan, we are asked to believe, is really a scholar and athlete named Lord Paddington, but has lost his memory after an accident. Restored to the aristocracy after a blow on the head, he retains the lowly Ollie as his valet. Eventually the Lord gets knocked on the head again, reverting to Stan, and the film ends with a happy reunion.

One of the truly legendary characters of the cinema, W. C. Fields had been a travelling circus performer and a juggler before making his first film in 1915. But it was his stage performance as Eustace McGargle in 1923 which established the classic Fields prototype of the con-man, tippler and loafer with a dislike of dogs and children.

The Bank Dick (Universal, 1940), a typically eccentric and inventive work made towards the end of his career, demonstrated that Fields in his sixties was still a match for any man, drunk or sober. In this picture, for which, as usual, he wrote his own script, Field is Egbert Sousé, trapped in a house full of aggressive, nagging females – wife, mother-in-law and daughter – the typical Fields hero. In the course of the film he catches a notorious bank thief, directs a movie and becomes a millionaire by shrewdly investing in some beefsteak mines. Finally he is installed in a splendid mansion, complete with butler, having earned the grudging respect of his family who now indulge his every whim.

SWASHBUCKLERS

Along with the musicals, comedies, gangsters and other escapist fare during the Thirties, there were the swashbucklers, with Errol Flynn, Ronald Colman and Douglas Fairbanks Jr. all carrying on the tradition which Fairbanks Sr. had made his own in the Twenties.

Based on the novel by Anthony Hope, **The Prisoner of Zenda** (United Artists, 1937), directed by John Cromwell for Selznick International, had already appeared in three silent versions, the most famous of them directed by Rex Ingram in 1922. Although the film was set in a mythical Ruritanian kingdom and conceived as pure fantasy, political ferment in the Balkans gave the intrigues at the core of the plot a certain topicality.

Selznick assembled a wealth of talent, including cameraman James Wong Howe, script-writers Donald Ogden Stewart and John Balderston, and a star cast – Ronald Colman, Madeleine Carroll, Fairbanks Jr., Mary Astor, C. Aubrey Smith, David Niven and Raymond Massey. Especially memorable is the final duel between hero and villain, here given new, original treatment (above). The fast, witty repartee of the adversaries is interspersed with each cut and parry of their sabres. And the likeably nasty villain – finely performed by Fairbanks – is allowed one last stylish gesture, a parting line, and a final dive into the castle moat.

Use of colour for the first time in such pictures as **The Adventures of Robin Hood** (Warners/First Inter-

national) and *Dodge City* in 1938 added a new dimension to the collaboration between Errol Flynn and director Michael Curtiz. It also reflected the increased prestige of Warners, now one of Hollywood's leading studios.

Aside from stunning photography and lively action sequences, *Robin Hood* boasted a fine cast. Eugene Pallette makes a delightfully eccentric Friar Tuck, Claude Rains is the wicked King John (in a red wig!), Alan Hale repeats his role as Little John from the Fairbanks *Robin Hood* sixteen years earlier, and Olivia de Havilland plays Maid Marion. Particularly splendid is the climactic battle when Robin (Flynn) is matched against his hated adversary, the villainous Guy of Gisbourne (Basil Rathbone), in an exciting duel to the death.

BRITISH LITERARY SUCCESSES

The best of British cinema during the mid- and late Thirties is reflected in a number of outstanding films taken from popular literary sources – Kipling, Shaw, Buchan and Wells.

Although loosely based on the John Buchan novel, **The Thirty-Nine Steps** (Balcon/Gaumont-British, 1935) is a typical Hitchcock movie, with the hero (Robert Donat) on the run from mysterious, sinister men, possibly enemy agents. The picture is virtually one long chase, on foot and by train, across country – an exciting formula, used in later Hitchcock pictures, designed to involve the audience with the action and to identify with the hero in his strange predicament, both frightening and bizarre, yet comical too (wanted for a crime he did not commit). Unable to go to the police, he must be wary of approaching anyone, since the most friendly-looking passer-by may be (and often is) in league with the enemy.

The extraordinarily fast pace, tensions and surprises of the plot, mingled with black humour, add up to one of the most amazing British films of the period.

The product of a somewhat unlikely collaboration between director Robert Flaherty and producer Alexander Korda, **Elephant Boy** (London Films) loosely derived from Kipling's 'Toomai of the Elephants', was filmed on location in India during 1935-6 and was completed at Denham Studios, with Zoltan Korda as co-director.

Although basically a Korda movie, Flaherty's major contributions included some marvellously authentic material, including the 'kheddahing' of the wild elephants in the stockade and the sequences between Sabu and his elephant. These are as good as anything in Flaherty's other films, anticipating the theme of his last film, *Louisiana Story* (1948). Unfortunately, his difficulties in working for Korda were similar to those experienced in Hollywood after the initial success of *Nanook* and *Moana* in 1926, although his collaboration with director Friedrich Murnau had resulted in one work, *Tabu* (1931), which was one of the outstanding films of the period.

Flaherty gave the lead role in *Elephant Boy* to a Mysore stable boy who had never acted before but turned out to be a real discovery – Sabu. The young star subsequently appeared in other Korda pictures, including *The Drum* (1938), the remake of *The Thief of Bagdad* (1940) and *The Jungle Book* (1942), before leaving Britain for Hollywood.

A landmark in the development of the science-fiction film, **Things to Come** (1936) was directed for Korda's London Films by William Cameron Menzies. The script was written by H. G. Wells from his book *The Shape of Things to Come*.

The film opens in London at Christmas when fears of an outbreak of war became a grim reality. Europe is devastated by a brutal and useless war in which the hero, John Cabal, is forced to take part. By 1966 Britain is governed by a ruthless chief (Ralph Richardson), but Cabal, now the leader of a society of scientists, manages to escape. Finally, in the year 2036, his grandson emerges as the benevolent leader who fires off a rocket to the moon, marking the first stage in man's conquest of the universe. The dual roles of Cabal and his grandson are played by Raymond Massey in one of his most authoritative film performances. The imaginative futuristic designs for the picture reflect the fact that Menzies was himself a former art director who had worked on the Fairbanks version of *Thief of Bagdad*.

51

Pygmalion (Pascal/General Film Distributors, 1938) was co-directed by Anthony Asquith and Leslie Howard, who also starred as Professor Higgins opposite Wendy Hiller's Eliza Dolittle. As with *My Fair Lady* twenty-five years later, the director aimed to preserve as much as possible of the qualities of Shaw's play. As Asquith stated, 'In transferring a play like *Pygmalion* to the screen, it is essential that the words should not be interfered with, and the problem for our team was how to provide a visual accompaniment to the dialogue which would give it its fullest effect.' This emphasis on dialogue and actors produced fine performances from the cast, especially Wilfred Lawson in the role of Eliza's father, the delightfully eccentric dustman.

Pygmalion was one of the high points in Asquith's long and distinguished career. Later he collaborated with playwright Terence Rattigan on such pictures as *The Way to the Stars* (1945) and *The Browning Version* (1951). Howard continued to combine acting and directing in a number of films, the best known being *The First of the Few* (1942), until his untimely death in 1943.

MGM PRESTIGE

During the late Thirties MGM shifted into top gear with a number of high-quality prestige productions – lavish musicals such as *The Great Ziegfeld* and *The Wizard of Oz*, love stories like *Camille* and *Romeo and Juliet,* and large-scale human dramas such as *San Francisco* and *The Good Earth*. Most famous of all, however, was a David Selznick production, in association with MGM, which borrowed the studio's top star (Gable) and a leading director (Victor Fleming) – *Gone With the Wind*.

The Wizard of Oz (1939) was MGM's answer to the enormous popular success of R.K.O.'s *Snow White* two years previously. A musical fantasy in Technicolor, based on the novel by Frank Baum, it tells the story of Dorothy, a Kansas farm girl, played by Judy Garland, whose attempt to save her pet dog leads to her getting caught up in a tornado and whisked off to the land of Oz. Her adventures with a scarecrow (Ray Bolger), a cowardly lion (Bert Lahr) and a tin man (Jack Haley) are preludes to her first encounter with the Wizard (Frank Morgan) and a dramatic confrontation with the evil witch (Margaret Hamilton). But, as in the best pantomime fairy-tale, all ends happily. The cast is excellent, the colour effective (if a bit garish at times), and the Oscar-winning musical score by Herbert Stothart, Harold Arlen and E. Y. Harburg contains more than a fair share of outstanding numbers, including 'We're Off to See the Wizard' and, of course, 'Over the Rainbow', sung by Judy. This is the film that turned her into a star.

The Great Ziegfeld (1936) linked two popular themes of the Thirties – the spectacular musical and the 'bio-pic' then in vogue. Clearly, Berkeley's accomplishments in the cinema, his geometric patterns of chorus girls and giant revolving sets, owe much to the Ziegfeld tradition in the theatre, and here the two are brought together.

The film won an Oscar, as did Luise Rainer, playing Ziegfeld's first wife (the shortest screen role to be thus honoured). It also reunited the *Thin Man* team of William Powell as Florenz Ziegfeld (below), and Myrna Loy. The picture traces the rise of Ziegfeld from his struggling days in show business to his greatest triumphs, providing ample opportunity for lavish production numbers. In the recently released tribute to the M.G.M. musical, *That's Entertainment* (1974), the film is represented by its most striking number – 'A Pretty Girl is Like a Melody', sung by Dennis Morgan, while a giant revolving staircase reveals a seemingly endless panorama of chorus girls, men decked out in top hat and tails, and Virginia Bruce perched far above at the summit.

Greta Garbo in the role of **Camille** (M.G.M., 1936) was,

according to director George Cukor, 'the happy meeting of an actress and a part.' The picture was the centrepiece of a trilogy of romantic/dramatic Garbo films, the others being *Anna Karenina* (1935) and *Maria Walewska* (1938). All based on nineteenth-century works of literature – *Camille's* source being the famous play by Alexandre Dumas – they provided Garbo at her prime with three of the best roles of her career. After 1938 she made only two more movies before retiring – *Ninotchka* (1939), a delightful comedy directed by Ernst Lubitsch, and *Two-Faced Woman* (1941), again directed by Cukor.

Although Garbo's portrait of a French courtesan appears somewhat romanticized, the picture works perfectly on its own, non-realistic terms. Little remains of the original play, but Garbo endows her part with a remarkable spiritual quality, aided by Cukor's sensitive direction and the talents of *two* leading Hollywood cameramen, William Daniels and Karl Freund. If Robert Taylor and Lionel Barrymore both seem rather weak as Armand, her lover, and his unsympathetic father – well, after all, this is Garbo's picture and she has never appeared lovelier on the screen. (See also page 28.)

54

Over the years **Gone With the Wind** (Selznick International/M.G.M., 1939) has acquired almost legendary status, the story of its making and subsequent success being as well known as the film itself. The original novel was written by Margaret Mitchell over a period of ten years, in complete secrecy. Producer David O. Selznick purchased the film rights in 1936 and spent two years putting together the final 'package'. George Cukor was to direct from a script by veteran writer Sidney Howard. Gable was the obvious choice for Rhett Butler but the casting of Scarlett O'Hara was more difficult. Some 1,400 possible candidates were interviewed and among the 90 who got screen tests were Joan Bennett, Susan Hayward, Jean Arthur and Lana Turner. Paulette Goddard was on the verge of being signed for the part when Selznick met a young English actress who was virtually unknown in the U.S. – Vivien Leigh. The rest is history.

Shortly after filming began, Gable objected to Cukor's direction and he was replaced by Victor Fleming. By the time the picture was completed a large number of directors, writers, designers and cameramen (all unlisted in the 'official' credits) had lent a hand, but the one man who made it all possible was Selznick. According to Olivia de Havilland, 'Only David kept it all in his head, overseeing the whole thing. He was the unifying force through the whole picture.'

Gone With the Wind was the biggest box-office success since *The Birth of a Nation* (another Civil War film) and the final notable achievement of Thirties Hollywood. But whereas the director D. W. Griffith had shaped the earlier picture, Selznick's domination of the later film reflected the power of the producer within the studio.

The presence of M.G.M.'s most popular stars, Clark Gable, Jeanette MacDonald and Spencer Tracy, undoubtedly contributed to the success of **San Francisco** (1936), nominated for an Oscar as best picture of the year, but beaten by *The Great Ziegfeld*. Directed by W. S. Van Dyke of the *Thin Man* series, the picture was produced and scripted by the husband and wife team of John Emerson and Anita Loos, who had worked on the first Fairbanks films twenty years earlier.

Gable plays the familiar part of a free-living saloon owner on the Barbary Coast, in friendly conflict with Tracy as a dedicated priest. With much of the movie confined to interiors, the story moves towards its climax – the great earthquake of 1906. The drama and destruction of the 'quake are brought to life on screen in a brief but effective montage sequence – unmatched in the cinema until the arrival of the vastly more elaborate and expensive production of *Earthquake* almost forty years later.

DISNEY

Walt Disney's first venture into the production of feature-length animated films during the late Thirties changed the face of the cinema.

The relase of **Snow White and the Seven Dwarfs** (Disney/R.K.O., 1937) marked the culmination of Disney's development as a producer of animated cartoons. He had been quick to take advantage of the coming of sound after 1928, introducing a new character, Mickey Mouse, and making his first use of colour in *Flowers and Trees* (1932). The market for short films, however, was limited and Disney took the plunge into feature-length pictures, despite the high costs and formidable production problems, in order to reach a wider audience. The bright colours of the shorts were judged unsuitable for an extended running time, so a more muted tonal range was devised for *Snow White*. Similarly, in order to sustain a more fully developed story line and preserve the individual qualities of the various characters, it was necessary to integrate the work of many artists and a small army of animators. The nastier, more violent details of the original Grimm story about the princess who arouses the jealousy of her wicked stepmother were toned down for a mass audience by diminishing the role of the evil queen

and emphasizing Snow White's life with the dwarfs.

The film's enormous success was not only a break-through for animation, with its emphasis on images and movement, sound and colour, but had a liberating influence as well on live-action movies.

Pinocchio (Disney/R.K.O., 1939), a children's story which, in the hands of the Disney Studio, acquired a visual style and distinction that could be appreciated by the most sophisticated adult, marked a notable advance on *Snow White*. The earlier film had not resolved the problem of animating a human character and its characterization of the dwarfs had veered towards sentimentality. Adapted from a story by Carlo Collodi, *Pinocchio* was generally darker in tone but better suited to the medium. The film describes the various different adventures of a wooden puppet who can walk and talk and needs no strings, but who keeps running into trouble despite the efforts of Jiminy Cricket to keep him on the straight and narrow path. Jiminy marks the first introduction into a Disney film of a little 'conscience' figure who reappears as Thumper the rabbit in *Bambi* (1943), Timothy the mouse in *Dumbo* (1941) and Tinker Bell the fairy in *Peter Pan* (1953).

Dramatic and entertaining, the film is also characterized by other visual/tactile qualities – the clean woody feel of clock- and toy-maker Gepetto's workshop, later eerily covered with cobwebs; a sudden flash of lightning turning the landscape silvery-white; the thick fog outside the saloon where Pinocchio is sold into captivity; the clouds of dust enveloping Jiminy as he rides on the wagon-axle; and the sea textures of the last reel when Pinocchio redeems himself by rescuing Gepetto from the belly of a whale.

The most 'experimental' of Disney's animated feature films made up of eight musical episodes conducted by Leopold Stokowski, **Fantasia** (Disney/R.K.O., 1940) took over four years to complete and involved more than a thousand contributors (character designers, story developers, special effects experts, etc.) and sixty main animators under the guidance of eleven directors. In some of the pieces a partial attempt was made to break away from total realism, and despite inevitable variations in quality among the different episodes the film remains a remarkable achievement. The most enjoyable and imaginative of the 'traditional' sections is 'The Sorcerer's Apprentice' (Dukas) starring Mickey Mouse, while 'Night on the Bald Mountain' (Mussorgsky) is notable for its powerful, vivid style and semi-abstract, almost surrealistic, depiction of demons, witches and evil spirits in mountainous hellscapes.

CHAPTER 3

THE WAR
AND AFTER

I'M DECENT I TELL YOU... NOBODY'S GOT NO RIGHT TO CALL ME NAMES!
THE PICTURE HOLLYWOOD SAID COULD NEVER BE MADE!
Hal Roach presents
A MIGHTY NOVEL! A SENSATIONAL STAGE SUCCESS!
NOW! THE YEAR'S MOST IMPORTANT PICTURE!
"OF MICE AND MEN"
by JOHN STEINBECK
with BURGESS MEREDITH · BETTY FIELD · LON CHANEY Jr.
Produced and Directed by LEWIS MILESTONE
Screen Play by Eugene Solow
Released thru United Artists
OF MICE AND MEN
A Novel by JOHN STEINBECK
AUTHOR OF "GRAPES OF WRATH"

LITERARY ADAPTATIONS

Outstanding literary adaptations during 1939–42 included *Wuthering Heights* and *How Green Was My Valley* from well-known British novels, and *Of Mice and Men* and *The Grapes of Wrath* from two of John Steinbeck's most famous works.

Of Mice and Men (Hal Roach, 1940) and *The Grapes of Wrath* were both based on novels by John Steinbeck about poor farm workers in the American West. The former is concerned specifically with the life of the migratory farm labourers of Southern California, and succeeds in capturing the feel of the Salinas River Valley where the story is set. Two workers – Lennie, the dim-witted giant, and George, his intelligent friend – share a dream of saving enough money to be able to buy a plot of land and settle down. But the film ends tragically when Lennie, unaware of his strength, accidentally strangles Mae, the wife of the boss's son, when she flirts with him. Lon Chaney Jr. gives the best performance of his career as Lennie – a role he had played on stage. Burgess

Meredith is excellent, although perhaps a bit too educated, as George, while Bette Field plays Mae. Directed by Lewis Milestone for producer Hal Roach, the picture features a memorable musical score by Aaron Copland.

The Grapes of Wrath (Zanuck/Twentieth Century-Fox, 1940), based on John Steinbeck's moving and compassionate novel about a Dust Bowl farming family who are dispossessed of their land and set out for California, makes no attempt to glamorize or soften the impact of the book. In fact some of the alterations, such as concluding the film with an impassioned speech by Jane Darwell as Ma Joad, may be regarded as definite improvements.

Asked what had attracted him to the subject, director John Ford replied, 'I just liked it, that's all. The whole thing appealed to me – being about simple people – and the story was similar to the famine in Ireland, when they threw the people off the land and left them wandering on the roads to starve. . . . I like the idea of this family going out and trying to find their way in the world.'

Superbly photographed by Gregg Toland before he made film history with his camera work in *Citizen Kane*, the picture also boasted outstanding performances from the entire cast, especially John Carradine as the preacher-cum-labour organizer and Henry Fonda in the leading role of Tom Joad. Jane Darwell and Ford both received Oscars. (See also page 62.)

How Green Was My Valley (Zanuck/Twentieth Century-Fox, 1941), also directed by Ford, depicts the tough life experiences of a Welsh mining community and the gradual changes which occur during the early years of the present century. As in *The Grapes of Wrath*, interest centres around the fortunes of a single family; but unlike the Steinbeck novel with its harsh contemporary realities, the Richard Llewellyn story is told in flashbacks, tending to soften and romanticize life in the Welsh village of his youth. This tendency is perhaps reinforced by the Hollywood sets (the village being reconstructed on the Twentieth-Century Fox ranch in the San Fernando Valley) and by the striking photography.

The acting is generally excellent, the cast including Roddy McDowell, Maureen O'Hara and the veteran British-born actor Donald Crisp, who won an Oscar for his performance as the father. Oscars also went to the picture itself, to Ford and to the film's cinematographers and art directors.

Based on the classic novel by Emily Brontë, **Wuthering Heights** (Goldwyn, 1939) was directed by William Wyler from a script by Ben Hecht and Charles MacArthur. With a largely British cast, including Laurence Olivier as Heathcliffe, Merle Oberon as Cathy and David Niven as Edgar, producer Sam Goldwyn spared no expense in trying to recreate the original Yorkshire setting locally in the grand Hollywood manner. Although much of the Brontë dialogue was retained, the picture is not too faithful to the spirit of the novel and is limited to the first half only. Yet it is beautifully photographed and well acted, its strengths and weaknesses best summed up in the words of cameraman Gregg Toland: '*Wuthering Heights* was a soft picture, diffused with soft candle-lighting effects. It was a love story, a story of escape and fantasy. So I tried to keep it that way photographically, and let the audience dream through a whirl of beautiful close-ups.'

COMEDIES

The studio tradition of the Thirties continued in many of the outstanding films of the early Forties, thanks to experienced directors like Hawks, Lubitsch and Curtiz, and to new directors such as Welles, Sturges and Minnelli, who introduced new ideas and injected fresh vitality into the old system.

His Girl Friday (Columbia, 1940) was adapted from *The Front Page*, a play by Ben Hecht and Charles MacArthur with an authentic Chicago newspaper background and based on real-life characters. Director Howard Hawks, uniting two popular genres, the newspaper picture and the screwball comedy, made on important change in casting ace reporter Hildy Johnson. 'I asked a girl to read Hildy's part, I read the editor and I stopped and said, "Hell, it's better between a girl and a man than between two men." I called Ben Hecht and said, "What would you think of changing it so that Hildy is a girl?" And he said, "I think it's a great idea," and he came out and we did it.' In the picture Hildy (Rosalind Russell) is torn between love of her newspaper and its ruthless editor (Cary Grant) and loyalty to her fiancé, the solid, dependable Ralph Bellamy.

A straight version of *The Front Page* had been made by Lewis Milestone in 1931; and in the most recent 1974 adaptation directed by Billy Wilder the leading parts are played by Jack Lemmon and Walter Matthau.

Filmed in colour and starring Judy Garland, **Meet Me In St Louis** (M.G.M., 1944) was the first real Minnelli musical, full of gaiety, vitality and movement. Adapted from the reminiscences of Sally Benson in *The New Yorker* magazine, the story presents a charming, nostalgic view of a St Louis family at the time of the 1903 World's Fair. As Minnelli has pointed out, 'The look of the film was based squarely on period shots of the town, and the costumes by Irene Sharaff were marvellously authentic.' The various numbers were carefully integrated into the story, such as the famous 'Trolley Song' which was originally 'just a number hanging in the air'. First attracted to the subject by the mock-horror of the Hallowe'en sequence, Minnelli managed to achieve something slightly off-beat. The picture is full of underplayed humour, such as the first appearance of little Margaret O'Brien clumping upstairs in her mother's too-large shoes and beginning a song, in a funny gruff

voice, which is carried on by grandpa and the girls in the carriage outside; and there is a tightly corseted Judy dressing for her first party. 'You look elegant,' remarks her sister. 'I feel elegant,' comes the reply, 'but I can't breathe!' Other Minnelli musicals of note include *The Pirate* (1948), *An American in Paris* (1951), *The Band Wagon* (1953) and *Gigi* (1958).

Preston Sturges's whirlwind career as writer-director at Paramount reached its peak in 1944 with the release of **Hail the Conquering Hero**, *The Miracle of Morgan's Creek* and *The Great Moment*. The 'hero' of the first film is a fraud, a would-be marine (Eddie Bracken) who has never dared tell the folks back home that he was rejected due to chronic hay fever and has spent the war working in a shipyard. A tough bunch of real Marines persuade him not to disappoint his mother by revealing the truth, and from the moment he arrives home, dressed in a

borrowed uniform and sporting a chestful of medals, there is no turning back: and the film continues, with many unexpected twists and turns, at a rattling pace.

A former script-writer, Sturges directed eight outstanding movies during 1940–4, his originality being reflected in satirical writing and witty, inventive dialogue. A director with tremendous pace and flair, he was able to draw excellent performances from his stars as well as from character actors such as William Demarest, Eric Blore and Franklin Pangborn, who acquired new stature in his films.

Lubitsch, undisputed master of sophisticated Thirties comedy, directed one last comic masterpiece – **To Be or Not To Be** (Lubitsch/Korda/United Artists, 1942). A black comedy dealing with the Nazi occupation of Poland, it has stood the test of time better than Chaplin's somewhat similar *The Great Dictator*.

A troupe of Polish actors, led by Jack Benny, put their talents for impersonating the Nazis to good use for the Polish underground. The success of the satire is due to Lubitsch's recognition and perceptive observation of the Nazis' basic absurdity, although he does not ignore the tragic consequences of the German occupation. This political theme is ingeniously interwoven with a marital farce concerning Benny's jealousy of his delightful wife, played by that superb comedienne Carole Lombard, who died in a plane crash shortly after completing this, her last, picture.

Lubitsch steps up the pace of the action and quality of the comedy as the film progresses, taking full advantage of the inventive script, witty dialogue and excellent performances by the entire cast.

RKO

Orson Welles's first pictures were made at R.K.O. in the early Forties, and the studio was also the home of Val Lewton, producer of a number of intelligent and original horror films.

Citizen Kane, directed by Welles for R.K.O. in 1940, is a real tour-de-force of the cinema. Drawing on his own theatrical experience, Welles wrote the brilliant script with Herman Mankiewicz and John Houseman. He then assembled a distinguished team of collaborators who, by means of long takes, deep focus effects, simulated newsreels, overlapping dialogue, distorted sound and trick photography, helped him extend the visual and aural possibilities of the cinema with breathtaking originality.

The lion's share of the credit must go to Welles, whose bravura performance as the newspaper tycoon Kane allowed him to dominate the film in front of, as well as behind, the camera. From the opening shots of Kane's death, with its extraordinary use of sound, lighting and photographic effects, one is plunged into a bizarre world, overwhelmed by sheer technical brilliance, and Welles's control hardly slackens during the next two hours.

Welles's next picture, *The Magnificent Ambersons* (1942), just as fine in its way, has always been overshadowed by *Kane*. Less flamboyant in style, but equally inventive in use of sound and visuals, the picture was taken away from Welles, substantially cut and re-edited; yet even in this form it deserves to be paired with *Kane* as a masterpiece of his early film career.

I Walked With a Zombie (1942) is one of the most fascinating and unconventional of horror pictures – product of an ideal partnership between director Jacques Tourneur and producer Val Lewton who made a series of high-quality, small-budget horror movies at R.K.O. during the early Forties.

A kind of reworking of *Jane Eyre*, set in the West Indies and concerned with voodoo rituals and native superstitions, the film is visually impressive and sensitively directed. The loose plot structure, with moments of suspense and horror suggested rather than made explicit, permitted Tourneur to concentrate on subtleties of mood and atmosphere. Although filmed in California, the West Indian night settings appear marvellously authentic; and the acting is generally of a high standard, with an amazing appearance by Darby Jones as a tall black zombie, and a notable contribution by a calypso singer named Sir Lancelot, composer and performer of the film's theme song.

US PRE-WAR

Before the arrival of a flood of American war films in 1944–5, most Hollywood 'prestige' pictures treated the subject in an indirect fashion. *Sergeant York* looked back at World War One; *Mrs Miniver* described the wartime life of a British housewife; *Casablanca* was set, none too convincingly, in North Africa; and *For Whom the Bell Tolls* romanticized the Spanish Civil War.

No film of the Forties better showed the advantages and disadvantages of the studio system than **Casablanca** (Warners, 1942), duly rewarded with Oscars for best picture, director (Michael Curtiz) and screenplay, with Humphrey Bogart and Claude Rains receiving nominations.

Little effort was made to conceal the picture's theatrical origin, with all action concentrated into a few days and centred around Rick's Café in a picture-postcard Casablanca manufactured in Hollywood. Dooley Wilson at the piano, sings 'As Time Goes By', Marcel Dalio supervises the gaming table, while Vichy Frenchman and Nazi (Rains and Conrad Veidt) are matched against Free

Frenchwoman (Ingrid Bergman), American (Bogart) and Czech patriot (Paul Henreid) – all the intrigue being counterpointed by a familiar story of love, duty and sacrifice.

This slick studio production – photography by Arthur Edeson, music by Max Steiner – has today become a cult movie, largely due to Bogart, and has recently been paid the ultimate tribute in Woody Allen's *Play It Again, Sam* (1972).

For Whom the Bell Tolls (Paramount, 1943) was the second major Hollywood film based on a Hemingway novel and here, as in *A Farewell to Arms* (1932), the lead was played by Gary Cooper. It is the story of an American fighting in Spain as a member of the International Brigade on the Loyalist side. Sent on a mission to blow up a strategically placed bridge, he joins a band of peasant guerillas in the mountains, led by Akim Tamiroff and Katina Paxinou, and has a brief affair with a young girl – Ingrid Bergman (right).

As in his two other war pictures of the period – *Sergeant York* (1941), for which he won his first Oscar, and *The Story of Dr Wassall* (1944) – Cooper effectively portrays the typical uncomplicated, peace-loving American, a kind of reluctant hero forced to fight in the cause of freedom. Cooper, Bergman and the picture itself were nominated for Oscars, while Paxinou won an Oscar for her supporting role.

BRITISH WAR FILMS

If World War Two can be said to have brought out the best in the British character, it also stimulated some of the finest film-making in the history of British cinema. There were outstanding pictures from new directors such as Jennings, Olivier, Lean and Coward, and from more established figures like Reed, Asquith and Powell.

Fires Were Started (Crown Film Unit, 1942) was the only feature-length documentary film by Humphrey Jennings whose career, more than that of any other director, was closely identified with the war experience. His first important work in films dated from 1939, while his other best-known pictures – *Listen to Britain* (1942) and *A Diary for Timothy* (1944) – both dealt with aspects of wartime Britain. Written directly for the screen, *Fires Were Started* describes the experiences during a single day of a group of firemen in the East End dockside area at the height of the London Blitz. Although most of the film is taken up by the highly dramatic, exciting and visually spectacular fire-fighting sequences in the docks at night, Jennings never allows his characters (firemen, relatives and friends) to be dwarfed by the action. As Lindsay Anderson has written: 'No other British film made during the war, documentary or feature, achieved such a continuous and poignant truthfulness, or treated the subject of men at war with such a sense of its incidental glories and its essential tragedy.'

In Which We Serve (Two Cities/British Lion, 1942) marked the directorial debut of David Lean and Noël Coward who went on to make several distinguished pictures together during 1944–6 (the former directing, the latter as author-producer), including *This Happy Breed*, *Blithe Spirit* and *Brief Encounter*.

In Which We Serve, in common with *This Happy Breed*, observes the impact of the war on the lives of people within a particular setting – in this case on board the destroyer *H.M.S. Torren*. Whereas in later collaborations Lean's influence was to emerge more strongly, in this film most of the credit must go to Coward. As Dilys Powell wrote in 1946: 'Noël Coward, the brilliant and irreverent English playwright, had been regarded in England and America as a man purely of the theatre. Elegant, cynical, he lived and breathed theatre: high comedy and drama, revue and musical romance. . . . In 1942 Coward appeared suddenly as a man of the cinema. *In Which We Serve* . . . was written, produced and co-directed by Coward; Coward wrote the music and played the part of the destroyer's captain. The film astonished a public accustomed to look on the author as the perpetual playboy.'

Directed by Carol Reed from a script by Eric Ambler and Peter Ustinov, **The Way Ahead** (Two Cities/Eagle-Lion, 1944) grew out of Reed's experience in shooting a short documentary recruiting film for the army, *The New Lot*, in 1942. *The Way Ahead* did for the army what *In Which We Serve* had done for the navy, following the fortunes of a new group of recruits. It is, however, a far better picture, obviously benefiting from a more experienced director, an excellent script and a fine cast led by David Niven (above), who had starred in Leslie Howard's *The First of the Few* two years earlier. There is a

natural progression from the early training sequences – depicted in semidocumentary style – to the dramatic journey aboard a troop carrier (torpedoed at night en route to North Africa), and finally to the initiation of the raw soldiers as they move into battle and come under fire for the first time.

Having won world-wide acclaim as an actor both on stage and in films – his most recent starring roles in the U.S. had been in *Wuthering Heights* (1939), *Rebecca* (1940) and *Pride and Prejudice* (1940); and, in Britain, in *The 49th Parallel* (1942) and *The Demi-Paradise* (1943) – Laurence Olivier chose **Henry V** (Two Cities/Eagle-Lion) for his debut as film director in 1944. This was the first major Shakespeare film since 1935–6 when three pictures had appeared in rapid succession, with varying fortunes – American versions of *A Midsummer Night's Dream* and *Romeo and Juliet*, and a British production of *As You Like It*, in which Olivier had starred opposite Elizabeth Bergner.

For this long-cherished project of bringing Shakespeare to the screen in colour, Olivier assembled a talented team, including cameraman Robert Krasker, designers Paul Sheriff, Carmen Dillon and Roger Furse, and composer William Walton; and in addition to playing the lead, Olivier helped Alan Dent to adapt the play for the cinema.

Olivier devised an ingenious opening, setting the scene in the Globe Theatre in Elizabethan London where the play is being performed on stage, then 'dissolving' out of the playhouse and backward in time to 1415. Apart from excellent performances by the entire cast, the picture is notable for its imaginative use of colour, most evident in the scenes of the opposing camps on the eve of Agincourt and in the actual battle sequences. The suspense reaches a dramatic climax with a travelling panoramic view of the charge of the French knights, advancing at the gallop toward the rows of English archers, and the release of thousands of arrows, causing chaos within the French ranks – one of the great moments in the cinema.

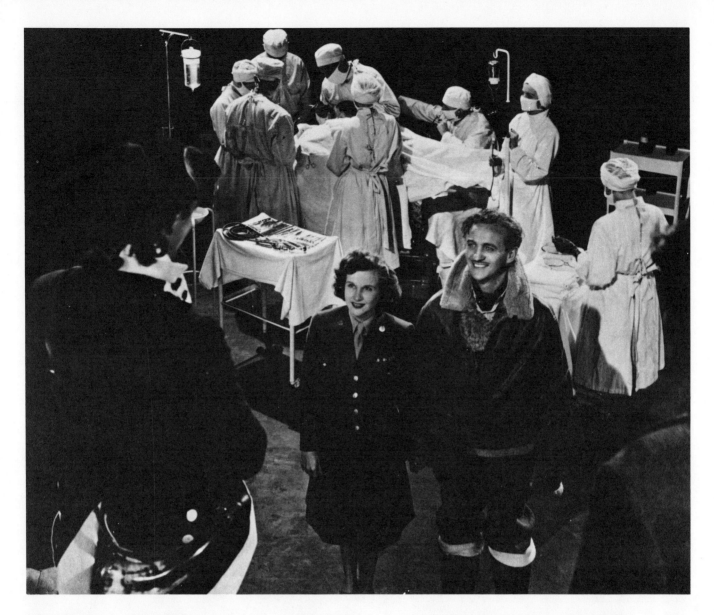

The last of the major British war pictures, **A Matter of Life and Death** (Archers/General Film Distributors, 1946) was begun during the last stages of the war in 1945 and was sponsored by the Ministry of Information, who were somewhat surprised at the result. The film opens with what appears to be a standard wartime situation – a battered plane limping back from a mission. But the scene is treated in an unrealistic manner, with strange and extraordinary shots of the burned plane and its occupants, culminating in the baling out of the pilot without a parachute.

The picture develops into a fascinating exploration of what goes on in the injured brain of the pilot (David Niven), a highly intelligent, sensitive man, suspended between life and death. The other leading role, that of a cultured brain specialist, is played by Roger Livesey who, as noted by Kevin Gough-Yates, '. . . is able to reveal to Niven, as the poet, the beauty of the earth in contrast to the dullness of the heaven of his imagination, while his brain-damaged mind rocks between the two.'

This picture, with *The Red Shoes*, represented the high point of the partnership between director Michael Powell and producer-writer Emeric Pressburger during the Forties, their other films including *The Life and Death of Colonel Blimp* (1943), *I Know Where I'm Going* (1945) and *The Tales of Hoffman* (1951).

US POST-WAR

Although the war theme hardly predominated in the U.S. to the same extent as in Britain, Hollywood did produce a number of outstanding war pictures, including *Air Force* (1943), *The Story of G.I. Joe* (1945), *They Were Expendable* (1945), *A Walk in the Sun* and *The Best Years of Our Lives*.

As one of Hollywood's last (and best) contributions to the war effort, **A Walk in the Sun** (Milestone/Twentieth Century-Fox, 1945) is notable for its restrained, anti-heroic qualities. Based on the novel by Harry Brown, with a script by Robert Rossen, the film concentrates on the experiences of a single platoon following the landing at Salerno in Italy in 1943. As in the closely related *The Story of G.I. Joe*, there were no big names in the cast, although Dana Andrews, like Robert Mitchum in the earlier film, was soon to achieve star status.

The picture was directed by Lewis Milestone, whose name was associated with war movies throughout his career. These included *The General Died at Dawn* (1936), *The North Star* (1942), *The Purple Heart* (1944), *The*

Halls of Montezuma (1950), *They Who Dare* (1953) and *Pork Chop Hill* (1958). This film, however, is the only one which matches his World War One classic, *All Quiet on the Western Front.*

Samuel Goldwyn got the idea for **The Best Years of Our Lives** (R.K.O. 1946) from a magazine article about ex-servicemen returning from the war, and commissioned MacKinlay Kantor to write the story, which was adapted for the screen by Robert Sherwood. The picture was directed by William Wyler who had made a number of 'prestige' films for Goldwyn over the previous decade. Here he was reunited with editor Daniel Mandell and cameraman Gregg Toland who, as in *Citizen Kane*, made effective use of compositions in depth.

The Best Years of Our Lives is shaped around a pattern of cross-cutting which follows the experiences of three returning servicemen – an army sergeant (Fredric March), a young flier (Dana Andrews) and a sailor who has lost both hands (played most movingly by non-professional Harold Russell). As Wyler wrote: 'The picture came out of its period, and was the result of the social forces at work when the war ended. In a sense, the picture was written by events and imposed a responsibility on us to be true to these events.' In this respect the film was an unqualified success, winning seven Oscars into the bargain.

MID-FORTIES THRILLERS

During the early and mid-Forties the thriller provided opportunities for comparatively new directors like Preminger, Huston (*The Maltese Falcon*) and Billy Wilder (*Double Indemnity*), as well as for old hands such as Hawks and Hitchcock.

Notorious (R.K.O., 1946), with a script by Ben Hecht, was perhaps Hitchcock's best film of the Forties and the finest of the three made with Ingrid Bergman during this period. Arriving in the U.S. in 1939, Hitchcock was to direct at least one picture a year for the next twenty years. But although his first American movie, *Rebecca*, won an Oscar as best picture of 1940, Hitchcock never gained an individual award – victim of the assumption that thrillers must be inferior to 'serious' pictures. This view was, to some extent, shared by Miss Bergman who, according to Hitchcock, '. . . only wanted to appear in masterpieces.'
  Notorious (left) ranks as a minor masterpiece, distinguished for its subtleties of character and relationship, and for the qualities of script, story and acting. From the

opening party sequence in which she is funny, sensual – and then taken in hand by Cary Grant, an American secret service agent who is scared half to death by her drunken driving, Miss Bergman has never been more radiant on the screen. The story revolves around the plotting of German agents and a cache of uranium hidden in wine bottles. In more ways than one, the picture was clearly ahead of its time, and Hitchcock only learned later that he had been briefly under surveillance by the F.B.I.!

Although Otto Preminger had directed a number of pictures before **Laura** (Twentieth Century-Fox, 1944), this film established his name and set the pattern for his subsequent career as a director of thrillers, which included *Fallen Angel* (1945), *Whirlpool* (1949), *Where the Side-walk Ends* (1950) and – best of the bunch – *Angel Face* (1952). In *Laura*, typically polished technique and fluid camera-work are matched by a literate, ingenious script and interpreted by a fine cast. Dana Andrews is the poor but honest cop investigating a murder that involves the cream of New York society. The underlying class elements are nicely sketched in as he is matched against a splendid collection of snobs, including Clifton Webb, Vincent Price and Judith Anderson, while Gene Tierney is the murdered 'dream girl' who suddenly turns up alive. The subtlety and restraint of the early part of the film gives way to an unnecessarily melodramatic and con-

trived climax, but the picture (left) is, on the whole, a fine example of its genre.

A kind of parody of the private-eye genre, **The Big Sleep** (Warners, 1946) is great fun – if a movie which includes seven murders and various other assorted brutalities can be so described. In his previous picture *To Have and Have Not* (1944), director Howard Hawks had first teamed Bogart with a new girl named Lauren Bacall, and the marvellous chemistry between them comes through even more effectively in this second picture. Based on the book by Raymond Chandler, Hawks's casual treatment of the plot gives the film a mysterious, unexpected, almost surrealistic quality. Even at the end not all the killings, disappearances and other strange events facing detective Philip Marlow are fully explained.

The unconventional style of the film is perhaps best summed up in Bogie's random encounters and amusing banter with various attractive women in the course of his investigations. A lady cab-driver, asked to do a 'tail job', replies, 'I'm your *man*'; and later, 'If you could use me again, call this number.' Bogart: 'Day or night?' She: 'Night's better, I work during the day.' As Andrew Sarris noted, 'The sexual repartee achieved an extraordinary frankness for its time in a Bogart–Bacall scene written in race-track parlance with Bacall observing that her performance down the home stretch depended on her jockey.'

BRITISH SUCCESSES

Revitalized during the war, British film-making continued to develop in the postwar period with a large number of distinguished productions from the same directors – Lean, Reed, Powell, Watt and Dickinson.

Brief Encounter (Independent Producers-Cineguild/ General Film Distributors, 1945) was the last of four films on which director David Lean collaborated with Noël Coward, who wrote the script as an adaptation from his own one-act play. It tells the story of Laura Jesson, a middle-class housewife, played by Celia Johnson, and presents that classic situation – the conflict between love, for a sympathetic doctor (Trevor Howard), and duty, as represented by her husband and family. And if it is difficult to connect such a story with the director of *The Bridge on the River Kwai* or *Lawrence of Arabia*, remember that Lean also directed some of the screen's outstanding

love stories from *Summertime* to *Dr Zhivago* and *Ryan's Daughter*. As always in Lean's movies, the acting is excellent, with occasional comic relief provided by Stanley Holloway and Joyce Carey.

The Overlanders (Ealing, 1946) was the first British feature to be filmed in Australia. According to director Harry Watt, previously best known for classic documentaries such as *Night Mail* (1936), *North Sea* (1938) and *Target for Tonight* (1941), 'I walked off the set of my one and only musical comedy, *Fiddlers Three*, to fly immediately to America en route for Australia to make a propaganda film on Australia's war effort. Having found the story of *The Overlanders* in the offices of the Ministry of Food, of all places, it took another six months to get it off the ground. I was allowed three production personnel from Britain; the rest we assembled from eager enthusiasts, from internment camps for German refugees, from sound recording studios, or just from the street. They turned out to be one of the most enthusiastic and cooperative units I have ever had.'

The picture is a kind of Australian Western, not unlike *Red River*, recreating the true story of a cattle drive across 2,000 miles of barren countryside which had occurred in

1942 when Australia feared an imminent Japanese invasion. Watt introduced the right note of documentary authenticity, and a fine, largely non-professional cast was headed by Chips Rafferty, himself a former drover.

David Lean followed *Brief Encounter* with two outstanding adaptations from the novels of Charles Dickens, **Great Expectations** (Falcon Films/Anglo-Amalgamated, 1946) and *Oliver Twist* (1948). In this pair of films he served Dickens as faithfully as Olivier had the Bard in *Henry V* and *Hamlet* (1948). All of these pictures, and *Great Expectations* in particular, demonstrate the solid literary foundations on which much of the best of British cinema during this period rested. The uniformly high standard of acting, not only of the leads – in this case John Mills as Pip and Valerie Hobson as Estella – but also the supporting roles, including Martita Hunt, Finlay Currie, Bernard Miles, Jean Simmons and Alec Guinness, is matched by the solid craftsmanship of cameraman (Guy Green), designer (Wilfred Shingleton) and director. Lean attempts to capture both the natural and the fantastic, making effective use of stylized sets, lighting and dramatic editing, as in the first startling appearance of the convict, Magwitch, in the graveyard.

The Queen of Spades (Associated British-World Screenplays, 1948), based on the story by Alexander Pushkin, was unique for its time in evoking the atmosphere of early nineteenth-century Czarist Russia, and all the more remarkable for being made on a tiny budget, with Thorold Dickinson, a last-minute replacement for another director, reworking the entire script during shooting. Appreciating the need for an imaginative approach, Dickinson admitted, 'After the first day I cast convention overboard and aimed in every scene at colourful, conscious contrast.' He gave high praise to his production team: 'When the story went out of doors there was always a wind blowing. The tempest evoked by the ghost of the Countess nearly blew the camera and its crew off their rostrum. Dust was thick as after a sandstorm. And Otto Heller's camera captured it all, while his camera operator Gus Drisse traced camera movements of outlandish and intricate composition. By juggling with camera lenses we also managed to give greater size and

contrasting scale to the sets which Oliver Messel designed and William Kellner built in two of the smallest studios in the country. In this epoch of neo-realism *The Queen of Spades* must have come as something of a visual shock.'

The story of **The Red Shoes** (Archers/General Film Distributors, 1948) was originally written by Emeric Pressburger for Korda before the war as a starring vehicle for Merle Oberon, with the idea of using a stand-in for the dancing. Director Michael Powell rejecting this approach decided that it was imperative to find a dancer-actress capable of handling the entire role – someone who could bring the necessary technical skill and emotional conviction to the part of the heroine of the specially created, twenty-minute ballet at the core of the film. In the event he selected Sadler's Wells ballerina Moira Shearer for the lead, and assembled an excellent cast of actors and dancers – including Anton Walbrook, Marius Goring, Robert Helpmann, Leonide Massine and

Ludmilla Tcherina.

The film works on several different levels. This is particularly noticeable in its treatment of motives concerning the complex relationship between life and art; and the creative process itself – its anguish and inspiration, its excitement and disappointments – has never been captured so well in a film. Strikingly photographed in Technicolor, with Oscars awarded to composer Brian Easdale and designers Hein Heckroth and Arthur Lawson, *The Red Shoes* is both exciting and moving; especially memorable is the extraordinary concluding sequence in which the ballet is danced without the heroine, now dead, a spotlight roving about the stage to suggest her presence.

Robert Hamer, the most stylish and sophisticated of Ealing Studios' directors, achieved international recognition as a writer-director with his **Kind Hearts and Coronets** (Ealing/General Film Distributors, 1948).

One of his aims, in his own words, was to make a picture '. . . which paid no regard to established, although not practised, moral convention, not from any desire to shock, but from an impulse to escape the somewhat inflexible and unshaded characterization which convention tends to enforce in scripts.' He succeeded, aided by fine high-key photography from Douglas Slocombe, and a superb cast. Alec Guinness gave a virtuoso performance as all eight members (both sexes) of the doomed D'Ascoyne family; and Joan Greenwood's bitter-sweet charmer was matched against Valerie Hobson's aristocratic beauty in vying for the affections of the scheming but sympathetic hero, played by Dennis Price.

Kind Hearts and Coronets, together with *Whisky Galore* and *Passport to Pimlico* in 1948, were the first great international, comedy successes of Ealing Studios, soon to be followed by *The Lavender Hill Mob* (1951), *The Man in the White Suit* (1952) and *The Ladykillers* (1955), all of which starred Alec Guinness.

According to Graham Greene, the original idea for **The Third Man** (London Films/British Lion, 1949) came from Alexander Korda who suggested that he should collaborate again with Carol Reed after their success with *The Fallen Idol* in 1948. Korda wanted a film about the four-power occupation of Vienna but allowed Greene to introduce a theme involving an unscrupulous character named Harry Lime. As portrayed by Orson Welles, Lime took on a highly individual flavour; and the stylistic similarity of the picture to Welles's own *The Stranger* (1946) and *Lady From Shanghai* (1949) suggested that he might have had a hand in directing it as well. Questioned about this in 1958, Welles replied, 'It's tricky to say anything about this film, because I've been very discreet. . . . All I can tell you is that I entirely wrote the role of Harry Lime. I created him all round.' Although he makes his appearance relatively late in the picture, Welles effectively dominates it in one of his most astonishing film performances. The atmospheric zither music of Anton Karas also contributed to the picture's great success.

WESTERNS

The Western took on a new lease of life during the postwar period in the hands of men such as Ford, Hawks and Vidor, evidently benefiting from the relaxation of studio controls and the tendency of most of the people under contract to want to do more filming on location.

My Darling Clementine (Twentieth Century-Fox, 1946), with Henry Fonda as Wyatt Earp, was the first Western directed by John Ford since *Stagecoach*. Ford had begun his career as a prop boy and assistant on a number of Westerns in 1914–17, and had met the real Wyatt Earp. Since 1926 he had virtually ignored the genre, but in this, the first of a group of postwar Westerns that included *She Wore a Yellow Ribbon* (1949), *Wagonmaster* (1950) and *The Searchers* (1956), he returned, as it were, to his grassroots as a director. Fonda, who had worked with Ford during 1939–40 on three pictures spanning American history and frontier life – *Drums Along the Mohawk*, *Young Mr Lincoln* and *The Grapes of Wrath* – brought the same quiet dignity and strength to the part of Earp as he had to his previous roles of Lincoln and Tom Joad.

The exterior set for the town of Tombstone was built at the edge of a desert, emphasizing its isolation in the wilds of Arizona; and the final showdown at O.K. Corral was carefully composed in accordance with Earp's personal account. In Ford's words, 'They didn't just walk up the street and start banging away at each other. It was a clever military manoeuvre.'

Duel in the Sun (Selznick International, 1947) set the pattern for those large-scale Westerns of the Fifties such as *Giant* (1956) and *The Big Country* (1958), which depicted the changing fortunes of a family dynasty of cattle barons. (See the following page.)

The voice of Orson Welles, heard in a brief prologue, referring to the legend of Pearl '. . . who was herself a wild flower, sprung from the hard clay, quick to blossom and early to die', gives early notice that this will be mythic

American cinema at its most flamboyant. Pulling out all the stops was that most flashy and dynamic of producers, David O. Selznick, who wrote the script and did his usual fast shuffle with different directors, cameramen, special effects men and 'second units', finally knitting it all into a relatively unified work, as in *Gone With the Wind* although that film had its own historic production story.

The picture enlisted the talents of some notable veterans of the screen – Lillian Gish, star of *The Birth of a Nation*, Lionel Barrymore, who had filmed with her under D. W. Griffith 45 years earlier, and King Vidor, director of *The Big Parade*; and the three leads were played by Gregory Peck, Jennifer Jones and Joseph Cotten.

Red River (United Artists, 1948), describing the first Texas cattle drive, soon after the Civil War, up the Chisholm Trail to Abilene, is firmly rooted in the myth and reality of the American West. As cattleman Tom Dunson, John Wayne enacts the larger-than-life character, the irascible yet sympathetic, weatherbeaten hero that he has since played in so many other fine Westerns. Here he is matched against a youthful Montgomery Clift in his first film role.

Although somewhat rambling and episodic, the picture preserves a feeling for character and relationships, played out against a broad Western canvas. Memorable sequences include the stampede of the cattle, an Indian attack, and the crossing of the Red River, filmed from inside one of the wagons.

Although director Howard Hawks had worked on *Viva Villa!* (1934) and *The Outlaw* (1943), this was his Western debut, as it was for script-writer Borden Chase. Both went on to make major contributions to Western films during the Fifties.

THRILLERS

Among the more unusual thrillers of the late Forties were Chaplin's black comedy *Monsieur Verdoux*, two pictures by Orson Welles and Robert Rossen's political thriller *All The King's Men*. But the main trend was towards greater realism, the films being adapted from true stories and shot on location, as in *Call Northside 777*.

Monsieur Verdoux (United Artists, 1947) was Chaplin's first picture for seven years. Clearly he felt it was time to abandon the popular tramp figure and this, his first true sound film, is a bitter yet amusing satire, loosely based on the story of the French murderer Landru, who preyed on rich, lonely ladies. As usual, Chaplin's own central performance (in which he dons a variety of disguises in order to escape detection) is amusingly versatile, but supporting roles are somewhat weak, apart from that of Martha Raye in a delightful episode which comes closest to the familiar Chaplin comedy vein.

The film suffered at the box office from the anti-Chaplin smear campaign engineered by the American right-wing press during the late Forties. Chaplin directed one last picture in the US *Limelight* (1952) – but his subsequent films, *A King in New York* (1957) and *The Countess from Hong Kong* (1966) were made in Britain.

During the immediate postwar period director Henry Hathaway made a series of thrillers filmed on exterior locations and sometimes based on true stories – *The House on 92nd Street* (1945), *13 Rue Madeleine* (1946), *Kiss of Death* (1947) and **Call Northside 777** (1947). In this last film James Stewart gives one of the best performances of his career as the dedicated reporter trying to prove that a man has been wrongfully imprisoned for a crime he did not commit. Here Stewart reveals the tougher, more mature side of his character, anticipating his emergence as a Western star during the Fifties.

Hathaway was working for Darryl Zanuck at Twentieth Century-Fox, which had now taken over films most closely associated during the Thirties with Warners. The studio's other great thrillers of this time included Elia Kazan's *Boomerang* (1947) and *Panic in the Streets* (1950), Siodmak's *Cry of the City* (1948), Preminger's *Whirlpool* (1949) and *Where the Sidewalk Ends* (1950), and Dassin's *Thieves' Highway* (1949) and *Naked City* (1950).

All the King's Men (Columbia, 1949), directed and scripted by Robert Rossen, was adapted from the Pulitzer Prize-winning novel by Robert Penn Warren based on the true story of Louisiana Governor and Senator Huey Long. Rossen had gained his first film experience as a writer at Warners, working on several socially conscious pictures and the first film he directed was *Body and Soul* (1947), starring John Garfield. For *All the King's Men,* his third picture, in opposition to the wishes of Columbia head Harry Cohn, he cast 'character' actor Broderick Crawford, rather than an established star, in the lead role of Willie Stark. Much of the picture was shot in Stockton, California, with local townspeople recruited for bit parts in an effort to capture the authentic feel of the original novel. The film had a good dramatic story and was well acted, although somewhat naïve and weak in its social and political implications. Nevertheless, the picture was a great success, winning both the New York Critics' and Academy Awards as best film of the year. Crawford, too, won an Oscar and was put under contract at Columbia, where his next important role, in *Born Yesterday* (1950), like his portrayal of Willie Stark, bore an unmistakable likeness to Harry Cohn!

The second phase of Orson Welles's career as a director during 1946–58 was a natural extension of his earlier work at R.K.O. Now the stylized and Expressionistic qualities, of *Citizen Kane* and *Journey Into Fear* in particular, were applied to a serious thriller format, as in *The Stranger* (1946), **Lady From Shanghai** (Columbia, 1949), *Confidential Report* (1955) and *Touch of Evil* (1958). Each film featured solitary and lonely men (not unlike Kane) portrayed by Welles himself. *The Lady From Shanghai*, although a somewhat uneven work, boasts a fine performance by Welles as an itinerant Irishman named Michael O'Hara and some superbly written dialogue, full of powerful imagery which complements that of the film's striking visuals. The sequence of a meeting between O'Hara and the beautiful but sinister heroine (Rita Hayworth) in the San Francisco aquarium was described by Welles as '. . . so gripping visually that no one heard what was being said.' Most memorable of all is the extraordinary chase through Chinatown and the final climax in a fun fair and hall of mirrors.

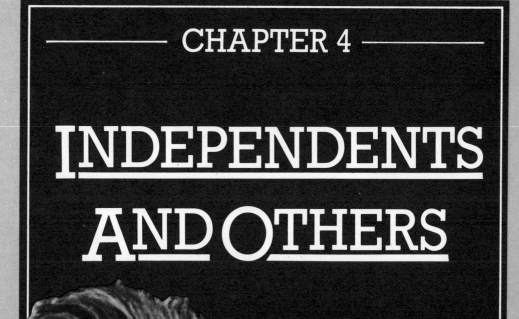

CHAPTER 4

INDEPENDENTS AND OTHERS

COMEDY AND MUSICALS

The comedy films of the early Fifties were dominated by two female stars, a veteran performer (Katharine Hepburn) and a newcomer (Judy Holliday); at the same time M.G.M. embarked on its great period of memorable musicals.

Scripted by Garson Kanin and his wife Ruth Gordon, and directed by George Cukor, **Adam's Rib** (M.G.M., 1949) was based on an actual situation involving two lawyers, husband and wife, on opposing sides of a divorce case. The Kanins saw it as an ideal vehicle for their friends, Tracy and Hepburn; and Judy Holliday was cast as the wife on trial for shooting her husband. Along with *Pat and Mike* (1952) – from the same writer-director team – *Adam's Rib* is the best of many pictures in which Hepburn and Tracy, close friends in real life, worked together. This delightfully witty comedy poses interesting questions about male–female equality and the 'double standard' imposed by society, qualifying as the first film about 'woman's lib', years ahead of its time.

On the Town (M.G.M., 1949) (right) was directed by Gene Kelly and Stanley Donen and based on a stage musical, in turn derived from the ballet *Fancy Free*, with music by Leonard Bernstein and choreography by Jerome Robbins. Kelly's individual style of dancing, based on broad, athletic movements, had been evident in *Cover Girl* (1944), his first picture as choreographer, in which a free-moving camera matched his acrobatic dance technique. But *On the Town* marked a real breakthrough for the musical form. In Kelly's words: 'After that, musicals just opened up. The fact that believable sailors got off a ship and sang and danced through New York was a turning point. . . . When we went to New York for location shots they (the studio) thought they were throwing their money away, but at least, when I insisted, they let me go ahead.'

New songs and music by Roger Edens and Comden and Green and a more elaborate story line than in the stage version provide the background for the dancing which projects an unabashed vitality and exuberance typical of the American musical at its best.

Based on his own hit play, the film version of **Born Yesterday** (Columbia, 1950) was skilfully 'opened out' by script-writer Garson Kanin who moved the action around the city of Washington (aided by some excellent location photography) without destroying the story's unity. Starring Broderick Crawford as a vulgar but wealthy scrap-metal dealer involved in Washington politics, and Judy Holliday as his scatterbrained mistress, this delightful comedy posed various censorship problems at the time. As director Cukor noted, 'It seems ludicrous now, but twenty years ago you couldn't have a character say, "I love that broad". And the nonsense that went on to get over the fact that Judy and Broderick were living together! . . . We managed to make it amusing, I think, but it was so unnecessary. Still, we kept in a lot of the important things regarding the heroine, a typical

"fallen woman", who'd lived with this rich man for years. But when she fell in love with William Holden and he kissed her, her reaction was virginal, as if she'd been kissed for the first time.'

The picture was awarded an Oscar, while Judy Holliday, cast for the lead largely on the strength of her performance in *Adam's Rib,* despite the misgivings of Columbia's head, Harry Cohn, won the best actress award over the two favourites (Bette Davis in *All About Eve* and Gloria Swanson in *Sunset Boulevard*).

Singin' in the Rain (M.G.M., 1951) reunited the team of *On the Town,* including Kelly and Donen (co-directors), Comden and Green (scenarists), and Harold Rosson (cameraman). It is a musical version of the popular back-stage Hollywood theme, examining with amusement the problems caused by the change-over from silent to sound pictures in the late Twenties. Kelly wrote of the talented team who collaborated with him on this and other M.G.M. musicals as follows: 'There was a group of young people, dancers, choreographers, producers, directors, a kind of repertory company we had there who were brought together from all over the country by a scouting system, like they have for football players. *Singin' in the Rain* is the best example of our musical group coming together. All we had was this old skit about a silent movie actor becoming a sound star. We all charged around the studios asking everyone what it was like in the old days. . . . Surprisingly, the only real difficulty was with the title dance sequence and explain-

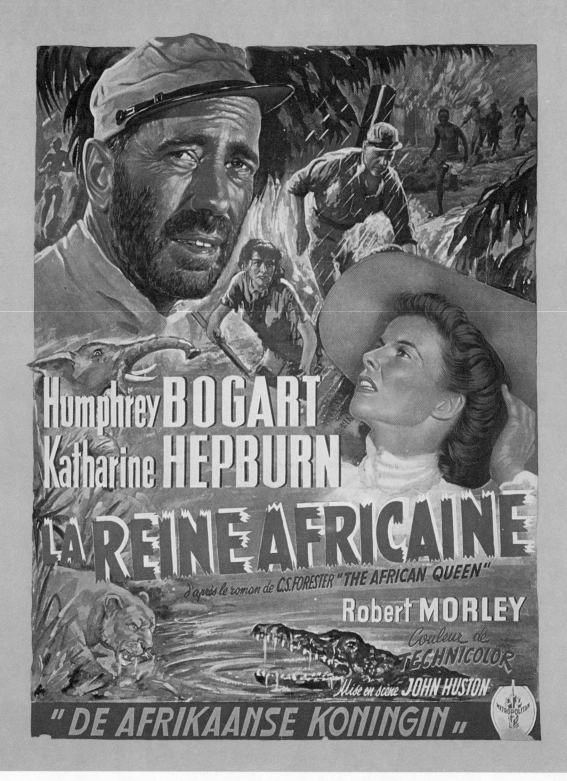

ing how it was to be done. Imagine me saying, "Well, I dance down the street in these puddles. . . .!" '

Apart from Kelly as the silent film stuntman who develops into a Fairbanks-style swashbuckler star, the film features Jean Hagen as the dumb-blonde female star who has trouble adapting (or being adapted) to the coming of sound, as well as Debbie Reynolds, Donald O'Connor and Cyd Charisse.

Based on the novel by C. S. Forester, **The African Queen** (United Artists, 1951) was directed by John Huston and starred Humphrey Bogart and Katharine Hepburn. Bogie and Huston had worked together on a number of pictures, including *The Maltese Falcon* (1941), *Across the Pacific* (1942), *Key Largo* (1948) and The

Treasure of the Sierra Madre (1948). The basically serious script by Huston and former film critic James Agee was lifted by this inspired casting, and indeed the nicely judged comic performances of the stars only emerged during the shooting (she was nominated for an Oscar and Bogart won one). The picture made unusual demands on the special effects department – realistic-looking leeches had to be designed to cling to Bogie in one sequence, while the shooting of the rapids was accomplished by using a miniature model and tiny likenesses of the stars. But when the script called for a swarm of attacking mosquitos, the specially bred insects refused to cooperate, a solution being found by stirring tea leaves into the clear water of a small aquarium, to the accompaniment of high-pitched buzzing on the soundtrack!

EARLY FIFTIES THRILLERS

After the first excitement of location filming wore off, the thriller film emerged stronger than ever during the early Fifties, combining old-style studio techniques and characterization with the best of modern methods, as shown by the contributions of leading directors such as John Huston and Elia Kazan.

Although the early career of Elia Kazan is generally associated with 'social problem' pictures such as *Gentleman's Agreement* (1947) and *Pinky* (1949), he admits that his first breakthrough to directing *films* rather than 'photographing plays' came with **Panic in the Streets** (Twentieth Century-Fox, 1950). 'We rewrote the script every day on location. That was the fun part of it. We were shooting in New Orleans and we had a hell of a time. I hung around the harbour and felt the wind on my face and thought: "I've been indoors all my life! I've got to get out of the theatre and into film!" '

The story dramatizes the dangers to the city when a dead body is found to be infected with the plague. Richard Widmark plays the doctor in charge of tracking down the source of the disease, which brings him up

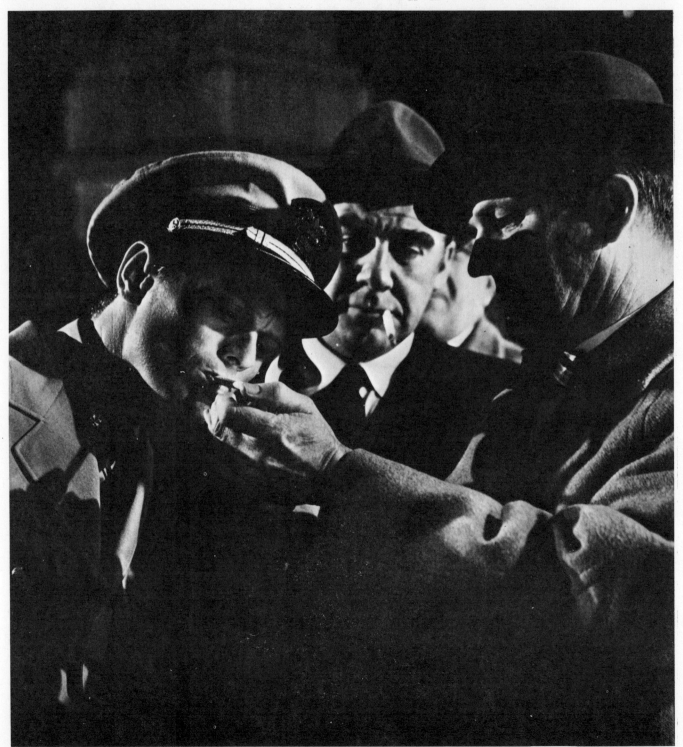

against a pair of ruthless underworld characters, played by Zero Mostel and Jack Palance. The picture is notable for its fluid camerawork and exploitation of the settings. And, like the best thrillers, it combines fast-moving action – including a chase climax – with good characterization. The brief sequences between Widmark and his wife (Barbara Bel Geddes) are handled with a sensitivity showing Kazan at his best. Widmark was ingeniously cast against type as the sympathetic hero, while the picture launched Jack Palance on his film career playing the first of that series of villains with whom he was identified during the Fifties.

The Asphalt Jungle (M.G.M., 1950) marked the culmination of John Huston's development as a director of thrillers during the Forties. But whereas the earlier films had generally featured an assortment of stars – Edward G. Robinson, John Garfield and Humphrey Bogart – *The Asphalt Jungle* was notable for its ensemble playing, suitable for the low-keyed, naturalistic style of the story – the careful planning and execution of a big jewel robbery. The opening shots show a police car roaming the deserted city streets, Sterling Hayden fleeing on foot, taking refuge in a roadside café, ditching his gun, then being arrested and shoved into a police identity line-up – all presented in a matter-of-fact style which sets the tone for the rest of the picture. The film is also notable for a brief but effective appearance by Marilyn Monroe in one of her earliest roles, while Jean Hager gives a moving performance as Sterling Hayden's hard-luck girl friend – (below).

BACKSTAGE DRAMA

The continuing decline of the old studio system during the early Fifties apparently stimulated an unusually large number of interesting 'behind-the-scenes' pictures about life in Hollywood including *Sunset Boulevard* (1950), *Singin' in the Rain* (1951), *The Star* (1952), *The Bad and the Beautiful* (1952), *The Barefoot Contessa* (1954) and *The Big Knife* (1955).

All About Eve (Twentieth Century-Fox, 1950) brought together two outstanding talents in writer-director-producer Joseph Mankiewicz and actress Bette Davis, who was offered the lead role only two weeks before the start of shooting as a replacement for the injured Claudette Colbert. Davis, celebrated for strong dramatic performances, was ideally cast as Margo Channing, the ageing actress whose strengths and weaknesses, neuroses and anxieties, are revealed at a critical stage in her life. The somewhat 'literary' quality of the final film reflects Mankiewicz's great respect for the written word and his preference for developing ideas at script stage: 'By and large, major deviations are rarely improvements when arrived at under pressure, off-the-cuff.' Thus the picture adheres closely to the witty shooting script: 'My original concept of *All About Eve* was, and remained, to tell a satiric tale of theatre folk, utilizing the flashback techniques within a satirical framework of the presentation and acceptance of that theatrical totem known as The Award.' He himself had won Oscars as both writer and director for *A Letter to Three Wives* in 1949 and did so again for this picture.

The opening of Billy Wilder's **Sunset Boulevard** (Paramount, 1950) is stunning. The homicide squad, escorted by the wailing sirens of two motor-cycle policemen, arrives at a Hollywood mansion early one morning and fishes out the corpse of a young man (William Holden) floating face-down in the swimming pool, while the voice of the dead man is heard recounting his story. (According to Wilder, the picture originally opened with Holden introducing himself from a slab in the morgue, but audiences found this so hilarious it was changed.)

A masterpiece of black humour, the story is about a hard-up screen-writer who accepts an invitation to live with a 'filthy rich' and slightly mad silent film star, played to the hilt by Gloria Swanson. Erich von Stroheim gives a fine, restrained performance as her butler and former director – he had actually directed Swanson in her last silent film, *Queen Kelly*, in 1928; and there are brief appearances from Buster Keaton, Franklyn Farnum, H. B. Warner and Cecil B. DeMille himself, seen on the set of *Samson and Delilah*, which he was currently shooting at Paramount.

Like most films about Hollywood, **The Bad and the Beautiful** (M.G.M., 1952) is loosely based on real events and real people. Told in flashback form, the picture traces the rise and fall of a tough, ambitious Hollywood producer (Kirk Douglas), as seen through the eyes of various acquaintances, including a writer (Dick Powell), a star (Lana Turner) and a director (Barry Sullivan). Director Vincente Minnelli explained the origins of the film: 'The central figure is a composite of many people: Val Lewton was the inspiration for the scene in which Douglas points out that terror is far more frightening if you don't show the source of the menace; and some of David O. Selznick was in the part. The character of the drunken star whose father was a famous actor was based partly on Diana Barrymore; and we had Louis Calhern do a kind of imitation of John Barrymore's voice on a record.' When Minnelli directed Kirk Douglas ten years late in *Two Weeks in Another Town* after the demise of the Hollywood studio system, a clip is screened from *The Bad and the Beautiful* implying that they don't make films like that any more.

WILLIAM HOLDEN
GLORIA SWANSON
ERICH VON STROHEIM
Sunset Boulevard
BOULEVARD DU CREPUSCULE
Production
CHARLES BRACKETT
avec
NANCY OLSON
FRED CLARK
LLOYD GOUGH · JACK WEBB
Mise en scène
BILLY WILDER
C'est un film Paramount
Films Paramount
DE LAAN DER SCHIMMEN

EARLY FIFTIES WESTERNS

Three directors new to Westerns – Delmer Daves, George Stevens and Fred Zinnemann – made films in the early Fifties which were notable for their thoughtful, serious treatment of traditional themes.

Based on the novel *Blood Brother* by Elliott Arnold and directed by Delmer Daves, **Broken Arrow** (Twentieth Century-Fox, 1950) (above) was the first Western which attempted to portray the Indian on the screen with respect and compassion. Later examples included *Taza, Son of Cochise* (1954), with Rock Hudson, *Apache* (1954), with Burt Lancaster, and *Run of the Arrow* (1957), with Rod Steiger. *Broken Arrow* was Daves's first Western, set in 1870, and tells the story of an army scout (James Stewart) who tries to negotiate a peace treaty with the Apache leader, Cochise, played with quiet dignity by Jeff Chandler. The scout's love for a beautiful Indian girl, convincingly played by Debra Paget, has overtones of Romeo and Juliet. He is forced to overcome the suspicion and hostility of the Whites, who think that he is

in league with the Apaches; and it is only her tragic death in an ambush, in which Stewart is seriously injured, which finally brings peace between the two warring sides.

A rather undistinguished story was transformed by script-writer Carl Foreman and director Fred Zinnemann when making **High Noon** (United Artists, 1952). Since there were no women in the original, a major adjustment was necessary in order to provide Grace Kelly with her first starring role; but her fine performance was overshadowed by that of Gary Cooper, who won an Oscar for his portrayal of the resolute, courageous sheriff confronting four bandits at high noon. As noted by Zinnemann, 'I saw this film *not* as a comment on the American Western hero, but as an enormously important contemporary theme which happened to take place in a Western setting.'

The careful planning of the film was exemplified by the tight script and the close relation of action to running time. Even the photographic style was meticulously controlled: 'We were very careful to omit all clouds in our outdoor shots. In most Westerns beautiful cloud formations are considered *de rigeur*. But we wanted to emphasize the flatness and emptiness of the land, and inertia of everybody and everything. To contrast all that with the movements of the marshal, we dressed Gary Cooper in black, so that when his lonely figure went into the stark, bright stillness, his destiny seemed even more poignant.'

Based on the novel by Jack Schaefer, **Shane** (Paramount, 1953) is *the* romantic Hollywood Western, beautifully photographed in Technicolor. There are fine performances from an all-star cast, particularly Van Heflin and Jean Arthur as the homesteader couple, Jack Palance as the hired gun, and Alan Ladd as Shane. As in the novel, events are seen through the eyes of the young boy (Brandon de Wilde) but director George Stevens cleverly used the picturesque setting as a means of expanding the original story to include some striking exterior action sequences. A good example of an event only referred to at second hand in the book is the dramatic death of Elisha Cook Jr., gunned down by Palance and yanked back by a specially designed, spring-operated harness at the point of impact. At the peak of his career during the Fifties, director Stevens is best remembered for his trilogy of Americana – an adaptation of Dreiser's *An American Tragedy*, retitled *A Place in the Sun* (for which he won an Oscar in 1951), starring Elizabeth Taylor and Montgomery Clift, *Shane*, and *Giant* (1956), from the Edna Ferber novel.

MARLON BRANDO

A new actor appeared on the screen for the first time in Zinnemann's *The Men* in 1950 and rocketed to stardom during the early Fifties, winning one Oscar and three nominations for performances in films directed by Kazan (*A Streetcar Named Desire*, *Viva Zapata* and *On the Waterfront*) and by Mankiewicz (*Julius Caesar* and *Guys and Dolls*). His name – Marlon Brando.

In **Julius Caesar** (1953), producer John Houseman and director Joseph Mankiewicz used all the resources of M.G.M. plus some British stars, yet sensibly decided to photograph their simple, functional Roman setting in black-and-white, not colour. Praised by critics on both sides of the Atlantic as the best Shakespeare film since *Henry V*, the picture was adapted from the relatively short play with almost no cutting. The result was an exciting, fast-moving and surprisingly topical 'political thriller' which avoided any film techniques or tricks which might distract from the actors and their lines. Performances are uniformly excellent, including John Gielgud as Cassius and James Mason as Brutus; but the chief laurels go to Marlon Brando for his stunning portrayal of Mark Antony. And if the film sags slightly in the second half, there is the suspicion that this is less the fault of the adaptors than of the original!

On the Waterfront (Columbia, 1954) is a powerful, dramatic film about corruption in a New York dockers' union, based, to some extent, on real events. Scripted by Budd Schulberg, with music by Leonard Bernstein, the story provided strong roles for Lee J. Cobb, Rod Steiger and Karl Malden, all of whom were nominated for Oscars. Yet their 'big' performances were overshadowed by the quieter playing of Brando in perhaps the best part

of his career. According to director Kazan, 'He would constantly come up with ideas that were better than the ones I had. I'd tell him what I wanted, he'd nod, and then he'd go out and do it better than I could have hoped it would be.' (Right).

The picture reflects the strengths and weaknesses of Kazan – a powerful, exciting and imaginative director working with bold strokes on a large canvas, but thereby missing some of those subtleties and complexities which might have made the picture more convincing in a documentary/political sense. Nevertheless it won no less than eight Oscars: those for best picture, best actor (Brando), director, supporting actress (Eva Marie Saint), cinematography (Boris Kaufman), script (Schulberg), art direction and editing.

BRITISH PRESTIGE

The diversity of British film during the Fifties is reflected in the following selection, which ranges from Ealing Comedy to Hammer Horror, from Olivier's Shakespeare to Halas and Batchelor's Orwell, with Jean Renoir's *The River* and John Ford's *The Quiet Man* in a class of their own.

Jean Renoir's film version of **The River** (United Artists, 1950) – the account of the daily life of an Anglo-Indian family – is based on the novel by the English writer Rumer Godden. Filmed on location in West Bengal on the banks of the Ganges, it has a quiet, intimate quality, underlining subtleties of character relationships, atmosphere and mood, and reflects Renoir's creative sensibilities. It was a truly international production, with an American producer, French director, cameraman and art director, Indian assistants and a cast of English and Indian actors.

Renoir, son of the Impressionist painter Auguste Renoir, arrived in the U.S. after the fall of France in 1940 and continued to use the same methods that had distinguished his earlier French films, their accurate portrayal of contemporary life being spiced lightly with social criticism. He still avoided using 'stars' and insisted on shooting such pictures as *Swamp Water* (1941), *The Southerner* (1945) and *The Woman on the Beach* (1946) on location. *The River*, his first colour film, looks back to his earlier works but heralds a new 'international' stage in Renoir's development – and is the first of a group of pictures reflecting a softer, more contemplative mood, including *The Golden Coach* (1952), filmed in Italy, *French CanCan* (1954) and *Picnic on the Grass* (1959).

The Quiet Man (Republic, 1952) is one of John Ford's most entertaining and enjoyable pictures, and the director himself no doubt identified with the theme of the Irish-American returning to the land where he was born. Although the exteriors were filmed on location in

Galway and County Mayo, Ford made little or no attempt to capture the authentic feel of Irish country life. For the humorous story is poetic and mythical rather than realistic, peopled by extraordinary, larger-than-life characters. John Wayne plays the title role of the peace-loving ex-boxer from Pittsburgh who buys the old cottage where he was born and is attracted to a local girl (Maureen O'Hara), thereby incurring the wrath of her brother, the squire (Victor McLaglen); and supporting roles are played by a number of colourful Irish 'character' actors led by the irrepressible Barry Fitzgerald. Action sequences include a local steeple chase and a marathon fight between Wayne and McLaglen. The film won Oscars for its striking Technicolor photography and for director John Ford.

The Tales of Hoffman (London Films/British Lion, 1951), based on the well-known opera by Jacques Offenbach, was the last of a series of large-scale pictures in colour on which director Michael Powell collaborated with writer-producer Emeric Pressburger. Apparently the original suggestion for the film came from Sir Thomas Beecham, who had enjoyed conducting *The Red Shoes* and wished to repeat the experience. One of the most successful adaptations of an opera to the cinema, *The Tales of Hoffman* was particularly notable for its striking decors and imaginative use of colour, drawing on the same design team of Hein Heckroth and Arthur Lawson that had worked on *The Red Shoes*.

Derived from the stories of the German author, E. T. A. Hoffman, the story follows the hero's amorous adventures – the prologue and each of the three episodes depicting his infatuation with a different beautiful woman. Hoffman is played by Robert Rounseville, but the acting honours go to Moira Shearer in the dual role of Stella and Olympia, Robert Helpmann – in the multiple part of Coppelius/Dappertuto/Dr Miracle – Leonide Massine and Ludmilla Tcherina; all of whom had appeared in *The Red Shoes*.

The Man in the White Suit (Ealing/General Film Distributors, 1952) was the first of two films – the second was *The Ladykillers* (1955) – in which the talented Ealing writer-director, Sandy MacKendrick, was teamed with the studio's leading comedy star, Alec Guiness. The story is of an employee at a textile factory who invents an indestructible fabric. But the picture's comic qualities shade into more serious satire as the implications of his discovery are explored; and the final shot of Guinness, when his white suit falls to pieces, achieves an almost tragic effect. Perhaps the most memorable feature of the film, however, is the extraordinary bubble-plop sound made by the white liquid brewing in Guinness's laboratory.

MacKendrick had made the highly successful *Whisky Galore* in 1948 and was later associated with such non-comedy films as *The Sweet Smell of Success* (1957) and *A High Wind in Jamaica* (1965).

The first Hammer version of **Dracula** (1957), directed by Terence Fisher, was more closely based on Bram Stoker's original novel than the 1931 Universal production starring Bela Lugosi, or Murnau's *Nosferatu* (1922). Rejecting the 'horror' label, and preferring to think of his pictures in a more 'romantic' sense as fantasy, fable, allegory or just plain 'macabre', Fisher treated Dracula with a certain degree of sympathy and compassion, later explaining: 'I've been accused of making him too material and not spiritual enough. But this is the mythology of Dracula; he has been doomed as a human being to walk the earth until such time as he is . . . released; he isn't destroyed. . . . He is a very sad figure, actually, because he is condemned to be a human being.'

A small production company which had recently ventured into the science-fiction field quite successfully with the Quatermass films (1955–6), Hammer had then turned to horror. *Dracula* and *The Curse of Frankenstein* (1957) both starred Christopher Lee and Peter Cushing.

Other notable horror films made by Fisher included *The Revenge of Frankenstein* (1958), *The Hound of the Baskervilles* (1959) and *The Devil Rides Out* (1967), the best of his later pictures.

Laurence Olivier's **Richard III** (London Films, 1955) is a highly successful and imaginatively conceived version of one of Shakespeare's early historical plays. Filmed in Eastman colour and wide-screen (VistaVision), it is not as outstanding an achievement as *Henry V*, yet is more satisfying than his *Hamlet* of 1948; and Olivier himself gives a stunningly original central performance as the malevolent humpbacked king. He again employed the talents of designer Roger Furse and of composer William Walton who had worked on the two previous films; and the fine cast included John Gielgud, Claire Bloom, Ralph Richardson, Cedric Hardwicke and Stanley Baker.

Olivier hoped to follow *Richard III* with *Macbeth*, but failed to find the backing. In the event, it was the Japanese director, Akira Kurosawa, who filmed *Macbeth* under the title *Throne of Blood* in 1951; although taking liberties with the text, this is perhaps the greatest Shakespeare film.

George Orwell's thinly disguised parable of the Russian Revolution, **Animal Farm,** was adapted by John Halas and Joy Batchelor as the basis for the first British feature-length animated film in 1954. A relatively simple, economical graphic style was used and the picture was also notable for its imaginative use of colour. The central situation is the rebellion of the farmyard animals against the cruelty of Farmer Jones; but the ending departs from the book in suggesting that they are now ready to revolt against the tyrannical pigs who have become their new masters.

According to Halas, '. . . the final story-board contained some 2,000 sketches for 75 minutes of action. These derived from a total of 10,000 sketches . . . an average of 26 drawings for each minute.'

Above, Animal Farm, *right*, Richard III

MUSICALS AND MARILYN

There were several interesting musical debuts during the mid-Fifties – Cukor directing Judy Garland in his first musical, *A Star is Born*; Brando and Mankiewicz making their first musical together, *Guys and Dolls* (1955); Audrey Hepburn in *Funny Face*; and Marilyn Monroe in *Gentlemen Prefer Blondes*.

A Star is Born (Warners, 1954) was the first in a decade of interesting musicals directed by George Cukor which included *Les Girls* (1957), *Heller in Pink Tights* (1960), *Let's Make Love* (1960) and *My Fair Lady* (1964); it was his first picture in colour. The film is one of those rare examples of a 'remake' that matches up to the original, although with the difference of being a musical. Here, as in the earlier version, the movie provided an ideal comeback role, in this case for Judy Garland, who, like Janet Gaynor, was nominated but failed to win an Oscar. It also presented her with a chance to extend her range, as Cukor pointed out: 'Until *A Star Is Born* she had only played musical comedy, but she was a very original and resourceful actress.' Her performance proved it, but unfortunately some of her best scenes, opposite James Mason, were cut, for the picture was considered too long. In the end a new 50-minute sequence, the 'Born in a Trunk' number, was added, making the picture longer than it had been and upsetting the overall balance.

Gentlemen Prefer Blondes (Twentieth Century-Fox, 1953) was a rare excursion into the musicals field by director Howard Hawks, and is remembered today as the picture which gave a necessary fillip to the career of Marilyn Monroe. Her performance as Lorelei Lee, famous heroine of the novel by Anita Loos (which had been turned into a stage musical) proved that Marilyn could sing as well as act. Darryl Zanuck, production head at Fox, where she was at that time under contract, was clearly unaware of her talents and was talked into casting her by Hawks. Hawks greatly enjoyed making the picture: 'In other movies you have two men who go out looking for pretty girls. We pulled a switch by taking two girls who went out looking for men to amuse them: a perfectly modern story. It delighted me. It was funny. Jane Russell and Marilyn Monroe were so good together that any time I had trouble figuring out any business, I simply had them walk back and forth, and the audiences adored it. . . . This type of movie lets you sleep at night without a care in the world.' (See also page 90.)

JUDY GARLAND JAMES MASON

WARNER BROS. PRESENT

A Star is Born

NEW SONGS *including* "THE MAN THAT GOT AWAY" · "IT'S A NEW WORLD" "GOTTA HAVE ME GO WITH YOU" · "SOMEONE AT LAST" · "BORN IN A TRUNK" TECHNICOLOR CINEMASCOPE

ALSO STARRING JACK CARSON · CHARLES BICKFORD WITH TOM NOONAN · SCREEN PLAY BY MOSS HART · DIRECTED BY GEORGE CUKOR · PRODUCED BY SIDNEY LUFT · NEW SONGS BY HAROLD ARLEN AND IRA GERSHWIN · A TRANSCONA ENTERPRISES PROD. · MUSICAL DIRECTION BY RAY HEINDORF · PRESENTED BY WARNER BROS.

The Seven Year Itch (Twentieth Century-Fox, 1955) was directed by Billy Wilder, who also collaborated with George Axelrod on the script, adapted from the latter's successful Broadway play. It is the story of the complications caused in the life of a middle-aged businessman (Tom Ewell) when a beautiful girl (Marilyn Monroe) appears from the apartment upstairs while his wife is on holiday. The role was much better suited to Marilyn's talents than those which the studio had been giving her and which had led to considerable tension on either side. Yet it contributed in a curious way to the break-up of her marriage to baseball player Joe Di Maggio.

Among the first sequences filmed on location in New York was a short street scene in which, as Marilyn passes over a grating, a cold blast of air from the subway lifts her skirt over her head – a refreshingly cooling experience which she evidently enjoys. One spectator on the set who failed to appreciate it was Di Maggio. A week later their marriage, already strained, was over. Marilyn took a break and later completed the picture, giving the best performance of her career and proving herself a gifted comedienne.

Directed by Stanley Donen, with songs by George and Ira Gershwin, **Funny Face** (Paramount, 1956) draws on the familiar theme of Americans abroad, featured in earlier Fifties musicals such as *An American in Paris* and *Gentlemen Prefer Blondes*. Here the story is set against the world of high fashion, with notable contributions from ace fashion photographer Richard Avedon, fashion designer Givenchy and *Harper's Bazaar* magazine. Stunningly photographed in VistaVision and Technicolor, with a witty script, the picture owes its success to the inspired casting of Fred Astaire and Audrey Hepburn. The seemingly ageless Astaire, paired for the third successive time with an actress-dancer of a younger generation – previously with Leslie Caron in *Daddy Longlegs* (1955) and Cyd Charisse in *Silk Stockings* (1957) – has never appeared more effective on screen in the multiple role of actor, dancer, singer and choreographer. And Audrey plays the 'dowdy, bookish, intellectual shopgirl' (in the words of the Paramount publicity blurb) who is discovered by fashion photographer Astaire and transformed into a sophisticated-looking model. It is no reflection on the picture to say that, given her natural radiance and charm, one might well have preferred her *before* she was thus 'transformed'.

THRILLERS

Despite the coming of television and the breaking up of the old studios, the relatively small-budget films – thrillers, gangsters and especially science fiction – continued to flourish in the mid-Fifties.

Swift-moving, tough, violent, superbly photographed and directed, **Kiss Me Deadly** (United Artists, 1955) has most of the virtues of the American thriller at its best and few of the defects. Foregoing the wit and charisma of previous private-eye types – William Powell as the Thin Man, Dick Powell and Bogart as Philip Marlowe – Ralph Meeker makes of Mike Hammer a truly frightening and ruthless character who refuses to let anyone or anything stand in his way. The picture is aurally and visually inventive, full of unorthodox cultural references ranging from Nat 'King' Cole and Schubert to classical opera and the poetry of Christina Rossetti.

Director Robert Aldrich was much indebted to script-writer A. I. Bezzerides who freely adapted the novel by Mickey Spillane and who also devised the idea of 'that devilish box', a kind of Pandora's box of the atomic age – the film's final dramatic revelation.

The Big Heat (Columbia, 1953) tells the familiar story of the honest cop (Glenn Ford) fighting against graft and corruption in a typical American city. A fast-moving, exciting thriller, stylishly photographed by Charles Lang, the picture's realism reflects the hand of Sidney Boehm, a former crime reporter, and has a clear relevance to the exposure of police corruption and gangster influence in American society at that period. On a deeper, more personal level, it deals with problems of individual responsibility, of justice and revenge, and of society's attitude to the 'criminal' – themes that had always preoccupied the film's director, Fritz Lang.

Lang was one of the leading directors of the German cinema during the Twenties and early Thirties; his early pictures included *M*, starring Peter Lorre, and the Dr Mabuse films. Arriving in the U.S. as a refugee from Hitler's Germany, Lang adapted his style and methods to the demands of the Hollywood system, beginning with two notable pictures – *Fury* (1936), with Spencer Tracy, and *You Only Live Once* (1937), starring Henry Fonda as a man wrongly convicted of murder.

The leisurely pace of Otto Preminger's **Anatomy of a Murder** (Columbia, 1959) appears to stem from the characteristically easy-going style of James Stewart's performance as the retired prosecuting attorney who is persuaded to take on the defence of a tough young army lieutenant (Ben Gazzara) accused of murder after learning of the brutal rape of his wife. The provocative sexuality of the attractive young wife (Lee Remick) is a key element in the drama; yet, surprisingly, a more mature, sophisticated actress was originally intended to play the part.

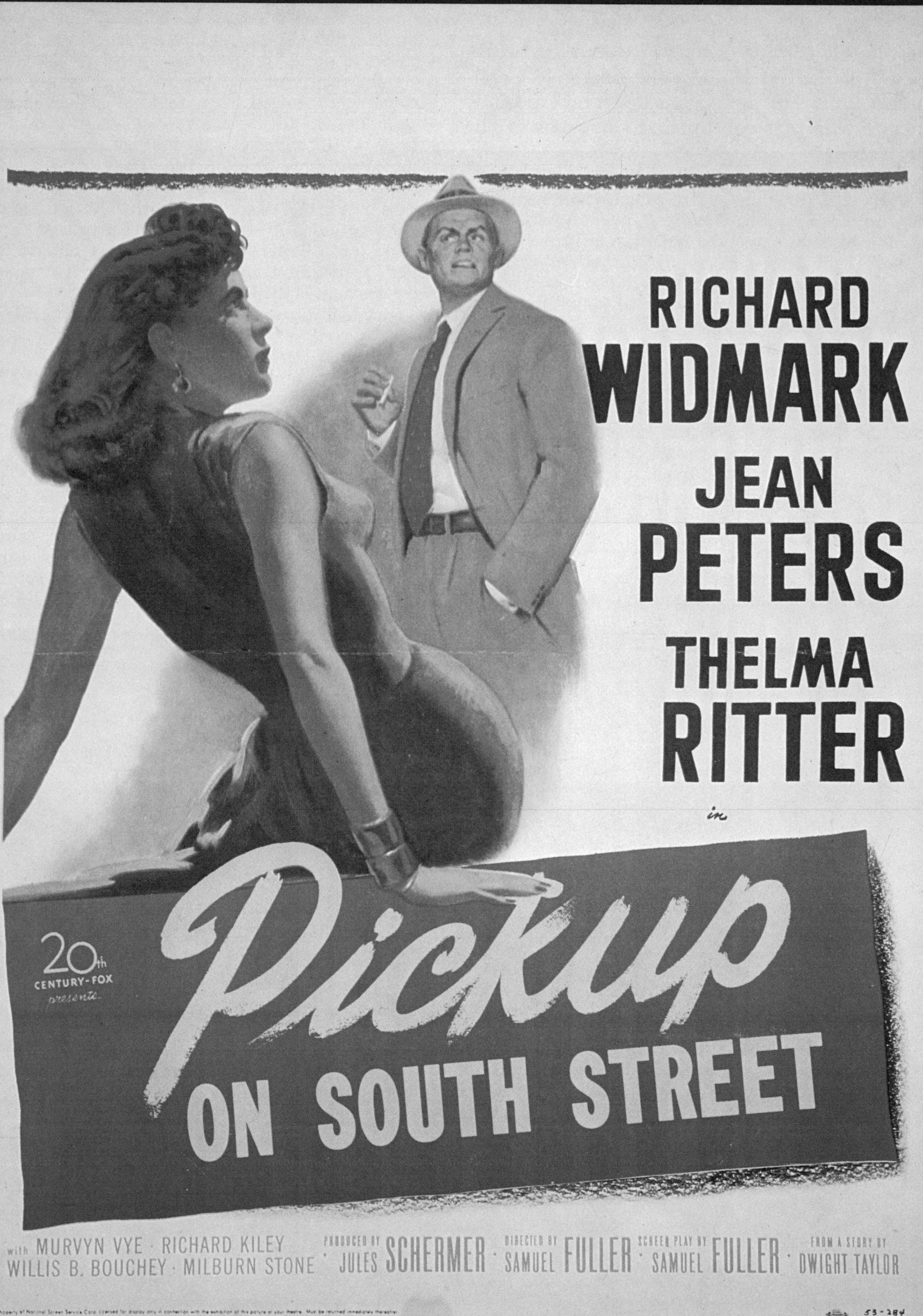
RICHARD
WIDMARK
JEAN
PETERS
THELMA
RITTER
in
20th
CENTURY-FOX
presents
Pickup
ON SOUTH STREET
with MURVYN VYE · RICHARD KILEY
WILLIS B. BOUCHEY · MILBURN STONE
PRODUCED BY JULES SCHERMER
DIRECTED BY SAMUEL FULLER
SCREEN PLAY BY SAMUEL FULLER
FROM A STORY BY DWIGHT TAYLOR
Property of National Screen Service Corp. Licensed for display only in connection with the exhibition of this picture at your theatre. Must be returned immediately thereafter.
Country of origin U.S.A. Copyright 1953 20th Century-Fox Film Corp.
53-284

According to Preminger, 'In the book the woman was older than the man. And I cast Lana Turner, but she wanted to have her costumes done by Jean Louis. I felt that the wife of a second lieutenant couldn't afford Jean Louis. So I signed Lee Remick.' The change altered the balance of the film and undoubtedly improved upon the original conception. The picture also presents an interesting variation on the theme of the honest country lawyer triumphing over the smart city-slicker, the latter role being excellently filled by George C. Scott in his first film appearance. Courtroom drama was a popular movie theme at this time, other notable examples including *Twelve Angry Men* (1957), *Compulsion* (1958), *Inherit the Wind* (1960) and *Judgment at Nuremburg* (1961).

Pickup on South Street (Twentieth Century-Fox, 1953) was the first of a series of gangster thrillers written and directed by Sam Fuller; others included *House of Bamboo* (1955), *The Crimson Kimono* (1959) and *Underworld U.S.A.* (1961). Fuller's individualistic, outspoken attitudes reflected his background as a journalist and crime reporter. As he said of *Pickup*: 'What I got a kick out of in the picture – the idea of having a pickpocket (Richard Widmark), a police informer (Thelma Ritter), and a half-assed hooker (Jean Peters) as the three main characters.'

The action, which occurs mainly at night in the subway and on dimly lit streets, is fast-paced, thanks to a mobile camera, quick cutting and an expressive use of camera angles. Filmed on location with great economy – the picture lasts only 80 minutes – the style is ideally suited to the subject. The performances, too, are excellent, with

Widmark in a familiar underworld role, Thelma Ritter in a nicely off-beat part, and Jean Peters (in a role originally intended for Marilyn Monroe) conveying authentic cheapness in dramatic contrast to her image of angelic beauty in *Viva Zapata* the previous year.

Rebel Without a Cause (Warners, 1955), directed by Nicholas Ray, is best remembered as the picture in which James Dean appeared in the role of the contemporary teenage rebel, the loner and anti-hero – the part which contributed most to the 'myth' surrounding Dean's memory. (See also page 91.) His performance in *East of Eden* (1955), from the Steinbeck novel, had turned him into a star overnight; and he was to make one more film, *Giant* (released in 1956) before his early death in 1955.

Filmed in Cinemascope and colour, *Rebel Without a Cause* followed on the heels of *The Wild One* (1954) and *The Blackboard Jungle* (1955), both dealing with themes of juvenile delinquency and teenage violence; but it was unique in trying to examine the causes of such behaviour, with particular attention to the 'generation gap' between parents and teenagers. And if the picture seemed excessively violent and melodramatic at the time, it has since been overtaken by events.

Don Siegel's **Baby Face Nelson** (United Artists, 1957) was perhaps the best 'B' feature of the Fifties – head and shoulders above the other 'public enemy' bio-pics of the period. Filmed quickly and cheaply from an excellent script by Daniel Mainwaring and Irving Shulman, the pace is fast and violent, reflecting Siegel's background as leading 'montage' expert at Warners during the early

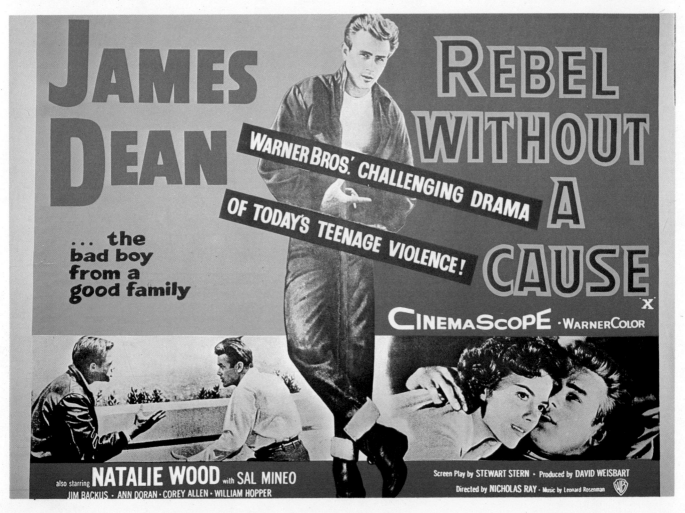

Forties. The theme, based on actual events, is familiar enough – the fugitive couple on the run. But the central characters of Nelson and his girl Sue, splendidly played by Mickey Rooney and Carolyn Jones, are portrayed in real depth. The force of their passion is powerfully suggested, never wavering until the bitter end when Nelson, fatally wounded, dies in Sue's arms.

In his first major gangster role, Rooney projects a convincing blend of toughness and nervous energy, dominating a cast of established Hollywood 'heavies' that include Ted de Corsia, Jack Elam, Leo Gordon, Emile Meyer and Elisha Cook Jr.

Other notable pictures made by Don Siegel in the mid-Fifties included the prison film *Riot in Cell Block 11* (1954) and a fine science-fiction movie, *The Invasion of the Body Snatchers* (1956).

SCIENCE FICTION

Space travel and invasion of the earth are the two science fiction motifs of the Fifties.

Forbidden Planet (M.G.M., 1956) is perhaps the most intelligent science-fiction movie of the Fifties. Filmed entirely within the studio, the strange landscapes and settings of a mysterious planet are convincingly brought to life, aided by a wide range of sound effects and electronic music.

The story is loosely derived from Shakespeare's *The Tempest*, with a fine performance from Walter Pidgeon in the central role of Dr Morbius/Prospero; and Anne Francis is provocatively innocent as the space-age girl who has never been kissed and who swims nude because she has never heard of a bathing suit, anticipating Jane Fonda's Barbarella. But the real star is Robbie the Robot, going about his duties with a pleasantly matter-of-fact attitude and deadpan voice – an obvious precursor of Hal the computer in *2001*.

The story also concerns an extinct civilization of high intelligence whose means of creating energy through the transference of mental power and thought processes have unexpectedly got out of control. This leads to a battle between the human characters and an invisible, seemingly omnipotent monster, which provides the film with its satisfyingly dramatic climax.

The War of the Worlds (Paramount, 1953) was one of a large group of science-fiction pictures during the Fifties which treated the theme of the invasion of the earth by alien, but not necessarily hostile, creatures. This film is loosely based on the H. G. Wells novel but updates and transfers the action from England to Southern California, where a Martian spacecraft, resembling a meteor, is first sighted. Other invaders land at various points on the globe and prove indestructible even when attacked with the most sophisticated modern weapons; but the earth is saved when they succumb unexpectedly to an invisible enemy – bacteria.

The expert use of miniatures and special effects is well demonstrated in the striking appearance of the Martians' domed war machines, firing deadly heat-rays, and in the convincing scenes of destruction that follow the invasion. The picture won an Oscar for its special effects.

Director Byron Haskin, producer George Pal, and art director Hal Pereira collaborated on two other sci-fi pictures at Paramount during the mid-Fifties – *The Naked Jungle* (1954) and *Conquest of Space* (1955).

LATER WESTERNS

A noticeable 'maturing' of the Western was evident during the late Fifties in the pictures of such veteran directors as Ford, Hawks, Anthony Mann and Delmer Daves, and in the playing of experienced Western stars – John Wayne, James Stewart, Walter Brennan and others. This trend continued into the early Sixties and found convincing expression in such pictures as *The Man Who Shot Liberty Valance* (1962), *Guns in the Afternoon* (1962), *Cheyenne Autumn* (1964) and *El Dorado* (1967).

The Far Country (Universal, 1955), along with *The Man from Laramie* in the same year, marked the end of the partnership between director Anthony Mann and actor James Stewart which had produced a distinguished series of Westerns and a number of other pictures in the early Fifties, such as *Winchester 73* (1950), *The Glenn Miller Story* (1954) and *Strategic Air Command* (1955).

The story of *The Far Country* concerns a Wyoming rancher and his grizzled old sidekick (Walter Brennan) who have driven their cattle herd to Seattle with a view to transporting the animals to Dawson City and then prospecting for gold. Stewart's rancher is a reluctant hero, a loner who takes pride in his independence and refuses to get involved in the violent affairs of Dawson City until he is bushwhacked and his friend killed. His final success in bringing law and order to the town recalls his only prewar Western role as the soft-spoken hero of *Destry Rides Again* (1939).

Described by director John Ford as 'the tragedy of a loner', **The Searchers** (Warners, 1956) provided John Wayne with one of his finest roles. It presents a harsher, more bitter view of the West than earlier Ford pictures, in which moral issues and conflicts appear simpler and more clear-cut. Yet it retains the same virtues – simplicity, strength and an almost classical purity; and it is

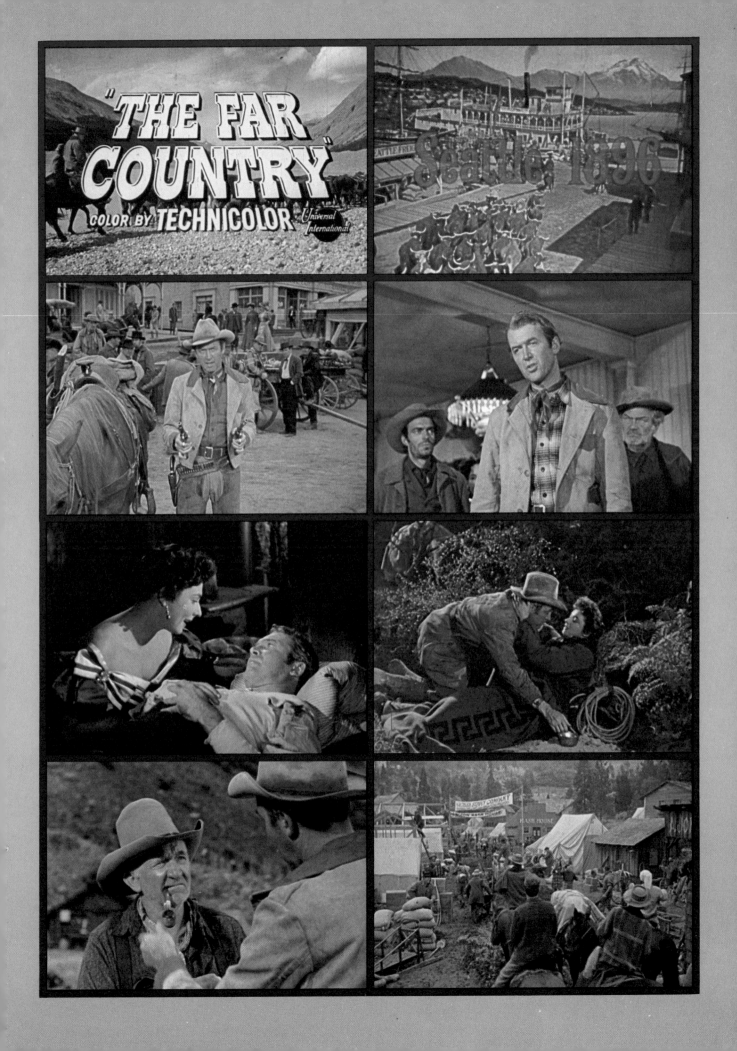

full of nicely understated moments, as in the sense of imminent danger suggested by a husband's quiet remarks to his wife before an Indian attack, or the hint that she is in love with his own brother. There are also some marvellous touches of humour, such as the wild fight between Jeffrey Hunter and Ken Curtis which disrupts the wedding – 'It was a nice wedding party, considering nobody got married' – or the striking appearance of Ward Bond as Captain the Reverend Samuel Johnson Clayton, sporting a fine moustache and battered top hat, identifying him as leader of the pioneer community.

3:10 To Yuma (Columbia, 1957) is an interesting example of the reworking of familiar Western motifs and situations, combining the theme of the struggle of the peace-living homesteader (Van Heflin) to establish himself and his family in the West with that of the lone lawman bringing an outlaw (Glenn Ford) to justice (see left). A blend of *Shane* and *High Noon*, the formula was successful enough to be reworked, with slight varia-

tions, in *The Last Train from Gun Hill* (1959). Director Delmer Daves's familiarity with the history of the West is reflected in his attempt to avoid romanticizing the story, placing major emphasis on his two central characters. The picture emerges as one of the best of the intimate, small-scale Westerns, deriving its power and excitement from the conflict between the characters rather than the action, of which there is comparatively little.

The central theme of **Rio Bravo** (Warners, 1959) is of a sheriff (John Wayne) holding a murderer in his jail, in defiance of the henchmen who are out to free him, until the arrival of the U.S. marshal. It thus unites the plots of *High Noon* and *3:10 to Yuma*, but with a difference, for it is directed by Howard Hawks, who here explores the

humorous side of a serious situation in an attempt to capture the kind of vitality and spontaneity of his earlier pictures. Thus Wayne – unlike the hero of *High Noon* who tries unsuccessfully to enlist the aid of the townsfolk – actually *rejects* the assistance of people who are not good enough with a gun and more preoccupied with the safety of their wives and children. And instead of going to meet his enemies armed only with a revolver, he uses both a repeating rifle and dynamite!

The cast includes Walter Brennan as the familiar garrulous old-timer, Dean Martin as an alcoholic ex-deputy, and Angie Dickinson as the delightfully aggressive heroine. The whole formula worked so well that Hawks repeated it some seven years later in *El Dorado* – one of the funniest Westerns of all time.

BLOCK-BUSTERS

In the middle and late Fifties television was steadily drawing audiences out of the cinema and back into the home. Pictures such as *The Ten Commandments, Around the World in Eighty Days, The Bridge on the River Kwai* and *Ben-Hur* made use of various wide-screen processes, exemplifying the attempt of the studios to meet this challenge.

As with their original production in 1926, M.G.M. chose Italy as the most economical and convenient location for the remake of **Ben-Hur** (1958), using the well-equipped Cinecitta studios on the outskirts of Rome. As a young man, William Wyler had actually assisted in the earlier picture. More concerned with characters and relationships than with spectacle, Wyler was aided in adapting the story by an impressive array of script-writers such as Karl Tunberg, Christopher Fry, Maxwell Anderson, S. N. Behrman and Gore Vidal. Wyler took pains to stress the friendship of Ben-Hur (Charlton Heston) and Messala (Stephen Boyd) in an early scene, pointing out that 'the love-hate relationship between the two men is what the piece is about.' And this interpretation even determined the final shape of the famous chariot race.

Although this sequence took months of rehearsal and was filmed in an arena with 8,000 extras, most of the race, as edited by Wyler, is seen in fairly close shots, emphasizing the individual conflict.

The picture won the unprecedented number of eleven Oscars, including those for best picture, director, actor, supporting actor (Hugh Griffith), music (Miklos Rozsa) and colour photography (Robert Surtees, using the newly developed 65mm Panavision cameras).

At the age of 73, Cecil B. DeMille embarked on the most ambitious picture of his long career, **The Ten Commandments** (DeMille/Paramount, 1956). The movie also proved to be his last, for he died in January 1959. Concentrating exclusively on the Biblical narrative (in contrast to the earlier version which had included a parallel modern story), DeMille planned to shoot all the exteriors on location in Egypt and the Sinai. He envisaged a budget of $8 million but the picture eventually cost about $13 million. However, it grossed four times that amount at the box office.

A star-studded cast that includes Edward G. Robinson, Vincent Price, Anne Bancroft, John Carradine, Yul Brynner and Cedric Hardwicke largely compensates for the weaknesses in the script, and Charlton Heston is especially impressive as Moses. Filmed in wide-screen VistaVision, the picture was a spectacular achievement and a worthy testament to cinema's greatest showman.

Around the World in Eighty Days (Todd/United Artists, 1956), adapted from Jules Verne's classic novel, was an ideal choice for the first venture into films of showman and impresario Mike Todd, who used the film to launch his own, improved wide-screen process known as Todd-AO.

Todd actually travelled around the world himself, persuading more than forty stars to appear in 'cameo' parts, including Marlene Dietrich, Frank Sinatra, Ronald Colman, Charles Boyer, Buster Keaton and Fernandel. In the four major roles, Shirley MacLaine appeared as Princess Aouda, Robert Newton as Inspector Fix, Cantinflas (the famous Mexican comedy star) as Passepartout the valet, and David Niven as Phileas Fogg. 'Elegant, imperturbable, Olympian,' in the words of script-writer S. J. Perelman, 'he strode across the world displaying utter aplomb at every obstacle man and nature interposed in his path. Each episode of the story heightened the momentum, irresistibly drawing you on, so that even though you knew the outcome you were enchanted.' Despite initial misgivings, Hollywood voted it the best picture of the year, with additional Oscars for the screenplay (by Perelman, John Farrow and James Poe), colour photography, music (Victor Young) and editing.

The Bridge on the River Kwai (Spiegel/Horizon/ Columbia, 1957), filmed in Cinemascope, was adapted from the novel by Pierre Boulle, itself loosely based on true events related to the building of the Burma Railway by British POWs during World War Two. Director David Lean's first war film since his initial co-directing effort on *In Which We Serve* in 1942 was awarded an Oscar as best picture of the year, as was Lean himself and star Alec Guinness (right).

The three main characters in the story are the fanatical commander of the British prisoners (Guinness), the harsh Japanese commandant of the camp (a fine performance by Sessue Hayakawa who was nominated for a supporting Oscar), and a cynical, opportunistic American prisoner (William Holden, in a slight variation of the role for which he had received an Oscar in 1953, in *Stalag 17*).

The film obviously took great liberties with the facts. Since the countryside around the real River Kwai was flat and uninteresting, the picture was shot in Ceylon. The Guinness character bore only the faintest resemblance to a real Colonel Toosey who had done much to ease conditions of British POWs in a camp in Burma. In suggesting, however, that the Japanese were incompetent engineers, the film grossly distorted the truth; and the climax of the picture, concerning the attempts of a sabotage team to blow up the completed bridge, was pure fiction.

HITCHCOCK

During the Forties and early Fifties the quality of Hitchcock's films tended to be somewhat uneven, the excellence of such works as *Notorious* (1946) and *Strangers on a Train* (1951) being balanced by the weaknesses of *Lifeboat* (1944) and *I Confess* (1952). But the master then produced an unbroken series of outstanding pictures which included *Rear Window* (1954), *To Catch a Thief* (1955), *The Trouble With Harry* (1955), *The Man Who Knew Too Much* (1956), *The Wrong Man* (1956), *Vertigo* (1958), *North by Northwest* (1959) and *Psycho* (1960).

In **Rear Window** (Paramount, 1954), one of Hitchcock's own favourites, James Stewart plays a photographer confined to a wheelchair with a broken leg, and the entire picture takes place in the courtyard adjoining the rear of his apartment, all events being seen through his eyes. Stewart believes that a murder has been committed and sends his girl friend (Grace Kelly) to investigate. The film's style is created largely through editing, cutting from close-ups of Stewart to occurrences in the yard.

The pacing of the picture, too, is carefully controlled. The rhythm gradually increases as suspicions mount, and the action builds up to an extraordinary climax as the killer attacks the helpless photographer, who tries to defend himself as best he can, even firing off flashbulbs to blind his assailant. Typical of the black humour running through the picture is the fact that, although Stewart is saved at the last minute, his *other* leg is broken, the final shot showing him still in his wheelchair, but with *both* legs in plaster.

Psycho (Paramount, 1960) represented something of a departure for Hitchcock, being the first of his series of those 'psychological-type' thrillers of the Sixties and early Seventies that included *The Birds* (1963), *Marnie* (1964) and *Frenzy* (1972), featuring a new generation of little-known actors rather than established stars. Filmed on a relatively modest budget of under $1 million and making use of television-style multiple camera techniques, *Psycho* was to be Hitchcock's greatest box-office success, grossing over $15 million.

The opening hour of the film is an absolutely riveting demonstration of Hitchcockian cinema at its most macabre, climaxed by the violent and unexpected murder of a girl in a shower. A textbook example of the use of 'montage', this scene took seven days to shoot and used 70 camera set-ups for a mere 45 seconds of film. Unfortunately, the rest of the picture is something of an anti-climax, and the final revelation of Anthony Perkins's character, with an elaborate explanation by Simon Oak-

land as a psychiatrist, is unconvincing. But maybe it is wrong to take the film too seriously and better to accept Hitchcock's own lighthearted attitude when he remarked, 'You see, it's rather like taking them through the haunted house at the fairground!'

Cary Grant in **North By Northwest** (M.G.M., 1959) (right) fits the bill as the typical Hitchcock hero – 'an average man to whom strange and bizarre things happen . . . the innocent fellow who gets involved in something he can't control'. And his talent as a smooth, unruffled comedy actor beautifully matches Hitchcock's unorthodox sense of humour. Like the heroes of *The Thirty-Nine Steps* and *Saboteur*, he is wanted for a murder he has not committed and spends most of the picture on the run both from the police and a sinister gang of foreign agents led by James Mason. The usual cool blonde heroine is played by Eva Marie Saint; and her role as a friendly agent in love with Grant, but also Mason's mistress, recalls that of Ingrid Bergman in *Notorious*.

The most memorable scene is the crop-dusting sequence. 'Crop-dusting where there ain't no crops,' someone remarks casually before Grant finds himself alone in a vast prairie landscape miles from anywhere and suddenly attacked by the low-flying biplane. There is also Hitchcock's favourite and disrespectfully incongruous use of familiar national monuments – a murder in the U.N. Building and the film's climax as hero and heroine scramble over the giant faces on Mount Rushmore with the enemy agents in hot pursuit.

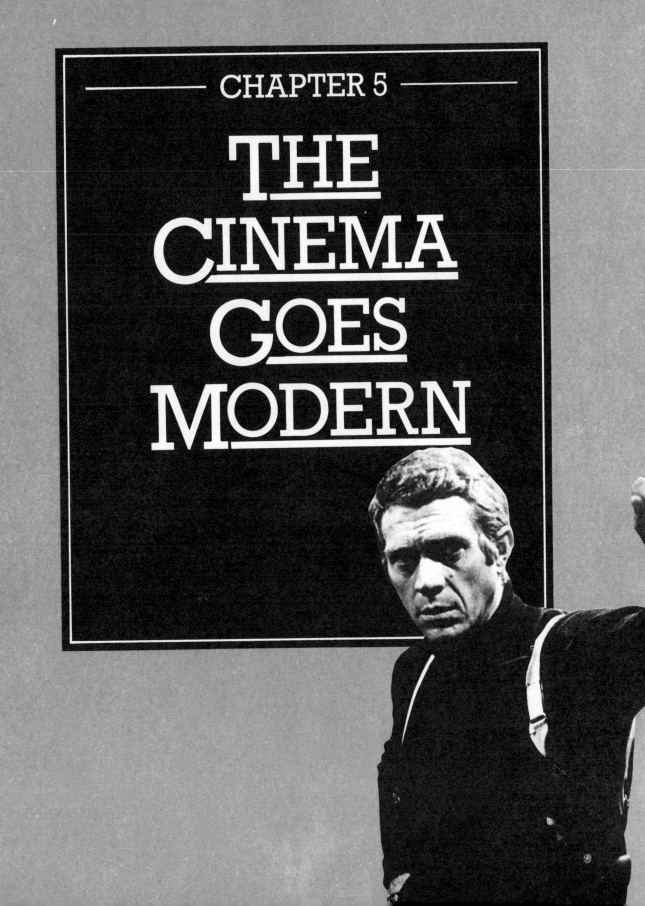

CHAPTER 5

THE CINEMA GOES MODERN

INTERNATIONAL HITS

The continuing efforts of the big production companies to compete with television led them to turn out a seemingly endless series of historical blockbusters during the early Sixties. In 1960 it was *Exodus, Spartacus* and *The Alamo*; in 1961 *El Cid, King of Kings* and *The Guns of Navarone*; in 1962 *Lawrence of Arabia, Mutiny on the Bounty* and *The Longest Day*; and in 1963 *Fifty-Five Days at Peking, The Fall of the Roman Empire* and, last but not least, the most expensive epic of all – *Cleopatra*.

In **Lawrence of Arabia** (Columbia, 1962) the partnership of director David Lean and producer Sam Spiegel brought to the screen the true story, intelligently scripted by playwright Robert Bolt, of the legendary T. E. Lawrence. Desert sequences were shot on location in the Middle East, giving them a particularly authentic feeling, and the various battles were especially striking. The Super Panavision, 70mm camera was marvellously effective in filming the chaotic scenes at an Arab camp

unexpectedly attacked from the air, the guerilla assault on a Turkish troop train, and the routing of the Turkish army at Akaba.

Inevitably, the characters tended to be dwarfed by the action, despite an all-star cast which mingled veteran performers such as Alec Guinness, Jack Hawkins, Claude Rains and Anthony Quinn with a pair of talented newcomers – Peter O'Toole as Lawrence and Omar Sharif as Ali Ibn El Kharish (both of whom received Oscar nominations). As with Lean and Spiegel's previous epic, *The Bridge on the River Kwai*, the picture won the top Oscar, Lean won the directing award, and other Oscars went to the art directors, to the cameraman (Freddie Young) and to Maurice Jarre for his memorable music.

The story of the making of **Cleopatra** (Twentieth Century-Fox, 1963) began in the late Fifties with an initial idea of a relatively small-scale picture featuring Joan Collins or Susan Hayward. The concept gradually escalated over a five-year period, with Elizabeth Taylor eventually being signed to star for a fee of one million dollars. Plans to do exterior filming in England, despite the unpredictable weather, led to the construction of giant sets which were never used. The original director, Rouben Mamoulian, was replaced after three months' filming in London by Joseph Mankiewicz, who also undertook substantial rewriting of the script. The entire production was removed to Italy but filming was again

halted when Liz Taylor fell dangerously ill with pneumonia. The final film cost $37 million but recouped a respectable $30 million at the box office.

Inevitably, *Cleopatra* proved something of an artistic disappointment. It is most successful in the first half when the young Cleo is matched against Rex Harrison's ageing Caesar and makes a triumphal entry into Rome on an enormous black Sphinx. Liz Taylor's attempt in the second part of the film to play a more commanding role opposite Richard Burton's Antony works less well, although the journey by barge to Tarsus has some spectacular moments.

Based on the best-selling novel by Leon Uris, **Exodus** (United Artists, 1960) was directed by Otto Preminger on location in Cyprus and Israel. This most solidly conceived of film epics, running three and a half hours, is notable for its realistic use of colour and for the performances of a star cast which includes Paul Newman, Eva Marie Saint, Ralph Richardson and Peter Lawford. In reconstructing the story of the birth of the state of Israel, Preminger carried out a considerable amount of background research prior to filming. Concerned to avoid turning out a 'propaganda film', he shifted the emphasis of the original book, trying to maintain a fair balance between the various warring factions and conflicting viewpoints involved; and in this respect the picture was reasonably successful.

MARILYN AND WILDER

The opening of the new decade was brightened by two highly original and entertaining comedies from writer-director Billy Wilder. Marilyn Monroe starred in one of these, but her other movie of this period, more sombre in mood, proved to be her last.

Four years after *The Seven Year Itch*, **Some Like It Hot** (United Artists, 1959) reunited Marilyn Monroe with Billy Wilder. He had written the original story and film screenplay expressly for her, being convinced that she was the only actress capable of projecting the blend of sexual provocativeness and innocence necessary for the character of 'Sugar Kane' Kowalczyk. A hilarious parody of the Prohibition era of the late Twenties, the story counterpoints its gangster theme – made particularly convincing and nostalgic by the presence of Edward G. Robinson and George Raft – with outrageous transvestite comedy. Co-stars Jack Lemmon and Tony Curtis are required to spend much of the film impersonating members of an all-female band, appropriate songs being included for Marilyn. There is no hint in the finished film of the anxieties and insecurities that made her so extremely difficult to work with in this instance, and her delightful performance turned out to be one of the best of her career.

A kind of fable for our times, **The Apartment** (United Artists, 1960), written and directed by Billy Wilder, is the story of a hard-working employee (Jack Lemmon) of a giant, impersonal insurance company who wins rapid promotion by lending his apartment for the nocturnal adventures of various executives. His career expectancies take a knock, though his personal prospects receive a boost, when one day he gets involved with a girl (Shirley MacLaine) left behind by a colleague.

The setting of the vast office, with its endless rows of desks stretching into the distance, was the work of veteran art director Alexander Trauner, who received an Oscar for his contribution. According to Wilder, 'the office was built in exact perspective. We had tiny desks at the back with dwarfs and then tinier ones with cutouts.' The film was one of the few comedies ever to win the top Oscar, and Wilder was awarded additional Oscars for his imaginative direction and off-beat script. His fruitful collaboration with Lemmon continued with such pictures as *Irma la Douce* (1963), *The Fortune Cookie* (1966), *Avanti* (1972) and *The Front Page* (1974).

The Misfits (United Artists, 1960), directed by John Huston (who gave Marilyn Monroe one of her early parts in *The Asphalt Jungle*) tells the story of proud men reduced to earning a living by capturing wild horses destined to be turned into dog food, and of a beautiful girl who has come to Reno for a divorce and stays on because she has nowhere else to go. At this time Marilyn's marriage to playwright Arthur Miller was coming to an end, but this, his first original screenplay, was written especially for her. Although somewhat literary in conception, it presented both her and Clark Gable with splendid roles, their performances alone being sufficient to raise the picture to the level of a modern 'classic'. Unfortunately it was to be the last film for both. Gable died of a heart attack, partially caused by the strenuous horse-roping sequences, shortly after the picture was completed; and Marilyn died less than two years later, having started another film, *Something's Got to Give*, which was never completed.

The cast also included Eli Wallich, Montgomery Clift (one of the latter's last pictures, too) and Thelma Ritter. Most memorable is the film's final action sequence of the pursuit and roping of a small herd of wild horses.

BRITISH PRESTIGE

Although the 'new wave' pictures were almost wholly British productions, most of the expensive 'prestige' films of the period, such as the James Bond movies and *Tom Jones*, were financed by the large American companies.

In contrast to the serious contemporary subjects of Tony Richardson's previous films in black-and-white, **Tom Jones** (Woodfall/United Artists, 1963), based on the classic eighteenth-century novel by Henry Fielding, was a light-hearted and entertaining romp in colour. Although Richardson saw it as 'a sort of Samurai – a thrilling adventure story and a protest against cant and hypocrisy', by the time filming was completed he was calling it 'the longest, most gruelling grind I've ever had. I feel I never want to do a costume movie again.' (Yet only a year later he was starting pre-production work for *The Charge of the Light Brigade*, which he directed in 1967.)

Broad and lively in style, *Tom Jones* used a wide range of filmic tricks and jokes, including stop-frame 'freeze' effects, jump-cuts, hand-held shots, wipes, silent film title inserts and speeded-up action. Albert Finney plays the hero whose wild escapades and sexual encounters –

including the celebrated orgy of eating with Joyce Redman – provide the picture with plenty of exciting action. A great success with critics and public alike, the film won the top Oscar, while additional Oscars went to Richardson, writer John Osborne and composer John Addison.

Dr No (United Artists, 1962) was the first of the James Bond thrillers, adapted from the stories by Ian Fleming. The series brought to the screen a kind of adolescent fantasy world, rooted in pulp fiction and adventure comic strips, yet with a universal and seemingly timeless appeal. The basic formula is unvarying – an assortment of sophisticated gadgetry, fast cars and faster women, nasty villains and plenty of action. The episodic plots hinge on the hero extricating himself from a sequence of apparently impossible situations; and everything is put together in a suitably slick, commercial package.

Terence Young, who directed three of the first four Bonds, clearly envisaged them from the start as a kind of send-up: 'The only way I thought we could do a Bond film was to heat it up a bit, to give it a sense of humour, to make it as cynical as possible.' The first Bond was Sean Connery, and *Dr No* also featured Ursula Andress, in bikini and sheath-knife, and Joseph Wiseman, memorably sinister in the title role.

The Bond series spawned an entire industry of Bond souvenirs during the Sixties and innumerable spy-thriller imitations, including *Our Man Flint* (1965), *The Ipcress File* (1965) and *Modesty Blaise* (1966).

BRITISH NEW WAVE

The pattern for the British 'new wave' of the early Sixties was set by Jack Clayton's *Room at the Top*, based on the John Braine novel, in 1958. Two early films in this category, both adapted from plays by John Osborne, were *Look Back in Anger* (1959) and *The Entertainer* (1960), directed by Tony Richardson; and he was also responsible for another stage adaptation, Shelagh Delaney's *A Taste of Honey* (1961) and *The Loneliness of the Long-Distance Runner* (1962), from an Alan Sillitoe story. The two best 'new wave' pictures, however, were *Saturday Night and Sunday Morning*, directed by Karel Reisz, and *This Sporting Life*, directed by Lindsay Anderson.

Room at the Top (Remus, 1958) represented a landmark in the development of the British cinema through its portrayal of life in a small provincial town, its exploration of such themes as class conflict and corruption, and its frank treatment of sex. It was the first feature film directed by Jack Clayton and it made the name of Laurence Harvey, playing Joe Lampton, the unscrupulous and ambitious young man from a working-class background who ends up marrying the boss's daughter. But it is French actress Simone Signoret, whose deeply felt, sensitive (and Oscar-winning) performance as the hero's rejected mistress helps to give real meaning to the film's moral statement – the high price paid by Joe Lampton for his social success.

Clayton's subsequent films have included *The Innocents* (1961), adapted from Henry James's *The Turn of the Screw*, *The Pumpkin Eater* (1964), from the novel by Penelope Mortimer, *Our Mother's House* (1967), from Julian Gloag's novel, and *The Great Gatsby* (1973), based on the novel by F. Scott Fitzgerald.

Saturday Night and Sunday Morning (Woodfall/Bryanston Films, 1960) was scripted by Alan Sillitoe from his own novel and directed by Karel Reisz, a former film critic who had made several shorts as part of the Free Cinema movement, in reaction against the unimaginative documentaries and class-bound features of the commercial British cinema. It provided Albert Finney with his first starring role as a good-natured, likeable working-class hero who resorts to practical jokes and pranks to relieve the monotony of a boring factory job and the tedium of home life. Highlight of his week is the Saturday evening visit to the pub, followed by a night of love with the wife (Rachel Roberts) of one of his workmates on night-shift. Far removed from Joe Lampton, this unrepentant, wild-living character has a vitality rarely seen on the British screen.

Reisz's later pictures have included *Night Must Fall* (1964), again with Finney, *Morgan, A Suitable Case for Treatment* (1966), *Isadora* (1968) and *The Gambler* (1974).

This Sporting Life (Independent Artists/Rank, 1963), based on the novel by David Storey and directed by Lindsay Anderson, is a uniquely powerful example of British 'new wave' cinema. Although Anderson retained the harsh realities of small-town competitiveness, as depicted in the book, he saw the picture as 'a study in temperament, a film about a man, a man of extraordinary power and aggressiveness, both temperamental and physical, but at the same time with a great innate sensitiveness and need for love, of which he is at first hardly aware, reflected in a very strange and complicated relationship with a woman'. Richard Harris is finely cast as the inarticulate rugby footballer, reeling from physical and mental pressures both on and off the field, and Rachel Roberts plays the woman in his life. Their intense scenes together, forming the core of the picture, were rehearsed for ten days prior to the shooting.

MUSICALS

The major musical successes during the mid-Sixties and more recently were designed to take advantage of a number of talented new female stars – Julie Andrews, Barbra Streisand and Liza Minnelli. The most successful British musical, however, was based on Lionel Bart's stage version of *Oliver*.

Jack Warner, head of Warner Bros, took personal charge of the production of **My Fair Lady** (1964), assembling the very best talent available. His well-publicized investment of $17 million paid off handsomely at the box office and walked off with most of the top Oscars, including those for best picture, director (George Cukor), set and costume design (Cecil Beaton) and best actor (Rex Harrison, recreating his famous stage role of Professor Higgins). Ironically, Julie Andrews, who had played the role of Eliza Dolittle on the stage, was passed over in favour of the more experienced Audrey Hepburn, but duly won the best actress award for *Mary Poppins*.

Filming in Hollywood, Cukor opted for a relatively conservative approach, but successfully captured on film those qualities that had made the Lerner-Loewe musical (based on Shaw's *Pygmalion*) one of the greatest hits of all time. As he explained, 'When you have these absolutely marvellous theatre scenes, there's no point in trying to tear the thing apart to make "cinema" out of it. You retain as much as you can and try to do it with a kind of fluidity.'

A delightful, witty and entertaining movie, **Mary Poppins** (Disney, 1964), based on the books by P. L. Travers, was made towards the end of Disney's life. It turned out to be his biggest box-office success and one of the top ten money-earners of all time. The film was something of a gamble for Disney, for it was a fairly expensive production that made use of elaborate special effects and required the world of Edwardian London to be recreated inside the studio. The picture combines a diverting story, songs, colour and sequences of live action blended with the movements of animated figures. Julie Andrews plays a kind of Super-nanny who flies in with her umbrella in response to the request of the Banks children and proceeds to put things right with the aid of her rather extraordinary magical powers before flying off again.

The movie was nominated for thirteen Oscars and won five, including the top actress award to Julie Andrews and another to Richard and Robert Sherman for their musical score.

The Sound of Music (Twentieth Century-Fox, 1965) was adapted for the screen from the stage musical by the well-known partnership of Richard Rodgers and Oscar Hammerstein. It was the last of a long series of successful musicals on which they had collaborated in the Forties and Fifties, including *Oklahoma*, *Carousel*, *South Pacific*, *The King and I* and *Flower Drum Song*. All had been turned into major films but *The Sound of Music*, filmed in the Austrian city of Salzburg, surpassed them all in box-office appeal. The story is based on the true experiences during the Thirties of the von Trapp Family Singers, the cast being headed by Julie Andrews who plays the young governess who loves to sing and daydream.

The phenomenal success of the picture at the box office, surpassing even that of *Gone With the Wind*, ensured the survival of Twentieth Century-Fox. Having been brought to its knees by the excessive cost of *Cleopatra*, the studio was now encouraged to invest a further $50 million in three blockbuster musicals during 1967 – *Dr Dolittle*, *Hello Dolly* and *Star* (the last a musical version, with Julie Andrews, of the life of Gertrude Lawrence). Both *Star* and *Dr Dolittle* flopped badly, ending the Sixties revival of interest in the lavish Hollywood musical and putting the studio back where it started.

Oliver! (Columbia, 1968), directed by Carol Reed and based on the stage musical by Lionel Bart (which was adapted from the novel by Charles Dickens), proved to be the biggest box-office success of any musical ever

filmed in Britain. In addition to the large and varied selection of spectacular production numbers typical of the modern 70mm musical, the picture preserves more intimate qualities associated with Carol Reed's early career. The feel of the rough, dingy back streets at night, covered with snow, resembles the setting of *Odd Man Out* (1947), starring James Mason and Robert Newton, who played a sinister Bill Sikes in Lean's *Oliver Twist* later that same year. (In *Oliver* the part is played by Oliver Reed, nephew of the famous director.) But most significant is the theme of the world as seen through the eyes of a child, which recurs in such Reed pictures as *A Fallen Idol* (1949) and *A Kid for Two Farthings* (1956).

Funny Girl (Columbia, 1968) was the first musical directed by William Wyler, adapted for the screen from the successful Broadway musical starring Barbra Streisand. Although she had never before appeared in a movie, the part was so closely identified with her that the producers decided to take a chance and star her in the large-budget film version as well. *Funny Girl* is loosely based on the true story of Fanny Brice, the Jewish girl from New York's East Side whose personality and talent as a comedienne and singer (rather than her looks) earned her star billing at the age of nineteen in the Ziegfeld Follies of 1910 and in many subsequent shows. Barbra Streisand's own background and career bear an obvious resemblance to those of Miss Brice, and her rendering of such traditional Brice numbers as 'Second Hand Rose' and 'My Man' has made them popular again

with modern audiences. Omar Sharif, playing the part of gambler Nick Arnstein, is rather dominated by Barbra but, after all, this is *her* picture and she won an Oscar for it. Within a year she was rushed into two other large-scale musicals – *Hello Dolly* and *On a Clear Day You Can See Forever* – and has since starred in a number of non-singing film roles.

Uncompromising in its representation of Berlin in the early Thirties, **Cabaret** (Allied Artists/ABC/Cinerama, 1972) is a distinctively modern film musical and the first to earn an 'X' certificate. With its powerful and effective use of cross-cutting to relate the cabaret setting to the broader events occurring in Germany at the time, the film marks something of a departure from the original stage production; and it is even further removed from the previous stage and film version, *I Am a Camera* (1955) and from the stories of Christopher Isherwood where it all began. If the Fifties adaptations were 'watered down' for censorship reasons, the film of *Cabaret* goes to the opposite extreme, dramatizing and making explicit those scenes which are merely hinted at or skimmed over in Isherwood's anecdotal sketches. This more forceful approach by director Bob Fosse is wedded to Liza Minnelli's tougher and more dramatic interpretation of Sally Bowles and is perfectly suited to the extraordinary appearance and performance of Joel Gray as the master of ceremonies. (All three won Oscars, as did the film.)

In mood, theme and setting the picture bears a close relationship to Fosse's previous film, *Sweet Charity* (1969), which takes place in a seedy New York dance hall.

THE US SCENE

The contemporary American scene provided the subject matter for a number and variety of interesting pictures in the early Sixties.

Based on the novel by Walter Tevis, **The Hustler** (Twentieth Century-Fox, 1961) was adapted and directed by Robert Rossen – his best picture since *All the King's Men* twelve years earlier. The film, largely shot on location and with non-professionals as the 'hangers-on', successfully captures the atmosphere of local pool halls with their assortment of amateurs, hustlers and big-time operators. The story matches Paul Newman as the up-and-coming, talented young player against the legendary Minnesota Fats (Jackie Gleason), the current undisputed champion. (A similar formula was developed, with rather less success, in *The Cincinnati Kid* (1965), with Steve McQueen challenging Edward G. Robinson in a marathon session of stud poker.) Their rivalry is exploited by a big-time manager (George C. Scott) and leads to a final gruelling confrontation. The picture is notable for outstanding performances by all three actors and by Piper Laurie as Newman's frail, unhappy girl friend – all four being nominated for Oscars. The veteran German cameraman Eugen Schufftan received an Oscar for his Cinemascope photography.

With its witty script and Hitchcockian blend of black humour and latent violence, **The Manchurian Candidate** (United Artists, 1962), (above) adapted from the novel by Richard Condon and directed by John Frankenheimer, was summed up by one writer as 'a comic nightmare on American family-cum-political life'. The central situation concerns a somewhat bizarre form of brainwashing which leads to a dramatic political assassination attempt at a Madison Square Garden convention. Frankenheimer's expressed aim was to expose the idiocy of political fanaticism both of the extreme Right and the extreme Left. Laurence Harvey is ideally cast as the zombie-like hero, while Frank Sinatra, Janet Leigh and Angela Lansbury are also outstanding.

The Manchurian Candidate and Frankenheimer's other thriller, *Seven Days in May* (1963) were but two of a notable group of American political films during the

early Sixties, including *Advise and Consent* (1962), *The Best Man* (1964), *Fail Safe* (1964) and *Dr Strangelove* (1963).

Stanley Kubrick's refreshingly disrespectful attitude toward the leaders of the two Big Powers with their nuclear war capabilities and 'strategic deterrents' is aptly summed up in the film title – **Dr Strangelove or How I Learned to Stop Worrying and Love The Bomb** (Columbia, 1963). In many respects it remains the best movie by an undoubtedly talented but uneven director, providing a nice balance between a satirical treatment of character and a fascination with gadgetry and 'mechanics'.

The precise structure of the film, based on cross-cutting between the besieged Air Force base, the lone B-52 bomber limping on to deliver its nuclear payload, and the Pentagon War Room with its assembled top brass, recalls the similar pattern of Kubrick's first major feature, *The Killing* (1955), about a carefully planned and executed race-track robbery. The mad generals and absurdity of official behaviour are reminiscent of his *Paths of Glory* (1957); and the strain of black humour best expressed by the appearance of Peter Sellers in multiple roles – as President Muffley, Group Captain Mandrake and Dr Strangelove himself – represents an appropriately bizarre use of this actor's talents, following the pattern of Kubrick's previous film, *Lolita* (1962). As Bryan Forbes put it, 'Kubrick has taken the Bomb and used it as a banana skin, with a nuclear pratfall as the pay-off.'

Loosely based on the Romeo and Juliet theme, **West Side Story** (United Artists, 1961) was co-directed by Robert Wise and Jerome Robbins, who had been responsible for the original stage production. Some of the sequences were shot on location in New York, including the long dance prologue which was introduced by some stunning aerial photography of the city. Robbins had definite ideas about blending choreography with a measure of realism, pointing out, 'It's rarely that a movie audience experiences the true force of the dance (the Michael Kidd ballets in *Seven Brides for Seven Brothers* being one of the few exceptions). What that audience does get, most of the time, is sex, charm, and daring, but not the genuine energy that dance should have.' This quality contributed immeasurably to the success of the film, which won the top Oscar, despite the fact that the vitality and originality of the dancing failed to inspire the rest of the picture.

BRITISH INDEPENDENTS

In marked contrast to the 'kitchen-sink' realism characterizing the British 'new wave', those pictures portraying the contemporary British scene in the mid-Sixties were notable for a freer and more stylized treatment. And whereas the earlier films had literary origins, movies such as *A Hard Day's Night*, *Cul-de-Sac*, *Blow-up* and *If...* were created directly for the screen. British cinema was further enlivened by various outstanding foreign directors, including Americans Joe Losey, Richard Lester, Stanley Kubrick, Roger Corman and Sidney Lumet.

Blow-up (M.G.M., 1966) is a genuinely international film – based on a short story set in Paris by the Argentinian writer Julio Cortazar, produced, directed and photographed by the Italian team of Carlo Ponti, Michelangelo Antonioni and Carlo di Palma, with an English cast and crew, and financed by the American production company M.G.M. David Hemmings plays the swinging young fashion photographer with more serious ambitions who, in the course of printing and blowing-up some outdoor snaps of a couple, suddenly realizes he has witnessed a murder attempt. Later, after an amusing 'orgy' sequence with two young girls who have been pestering him to take their photograph, he returns to the park to find a body actually lying there. Photographs and body are subsequently removed but the point is clear. The film is not nearly as vague or difficult as most critics have assumed, and is full of light and humorous touches. Antonioni is not asking, 'What is reality?' or suggesting the impossibility of distinguishing reality from illusion. Rather he is saying, 'Reality is strange', which is subtly but significantly different. A murder *was* committed, a body *was* there and has then been removed.

If... (Memorial Enterprises/Paramount, 1968) is an intensely personal work from director Lindsay Anderson which draws on his own experience and attitudes – as expressed in the Free Cinema movement – and which abandons traditional concepts of narrative construction and style. There is a clear progression in Anderson's work, from the 'subjective realism' of *This Sporting Life* to the mixture of fantasy and reality found in *If*... and then on to the extraordinary make-believe world of *O Lucky Man* (1974), which appears the weakest of the three films.

The fantasy of *If*... is firmly grounded at first in a realistic treatment of the film's public school setting, but tends to get progressively wilder as it develops, culminating in the final extraordinary and effective revolutionary outburst. The picture is a unique achievement within the British cinema tradition, yet not completely original, for it shows the strong influence of the French cinema (Godard, for example) and of Jean Vigo's Thirties classic, *Zéro de Conduite*, which provides the dramatic ending and some of the best visual jokes. Most notable among the group of largely non-professional players was Malcolm McDowell in the central role of Mick (right). McDowell subsequently starred in Kubrick's *A Clockwork Orange* and Anderson's *O Lucky Man*.

The Servant (Warner-Pathé, 1963) was directed by Joe Losey and scripted, from the novel by Robin Maugham, by Harold Pinter – their other collaborations being *Accident* (1967) and *The Go-Between* (1971). The picture is a black comedy which deals with the themes of class and master-servant relationships involving four central characters, well played by James Fox, Wendy Craig, Sarah Miles and Dirk Bogarde, who gives the best performance thus far in his career. Losey makes imaginative use of the Georgian house which serves as the stylized central setting. Having just returned to London and purchased the house, Fox takes on Bogarde as his manservant, and the sinister development of their relationship is paralleled by the gradual transformation of the house itself. According to art director Richard MacDonald, 'the idea was to get this old house, then to see it refurbished and properly furnished, and then (finally) to close in on itself until all the windows were shut and gradually all the curtains were drawn and no one went out, until it all became practically unbearable . . .'

A Hard Day's Night (United Artists, 1964) was originally envisaged as a quick attempt to cash in on the Beatles' success at the peak of their popularity. But by the time the production was set up and the script written, they had made their first American tour and become super-stars, thus ensuring the picture's success. Semi-documentary in style, the film follows the Beatles from their arrival in London by train through the 36 hours leading up to a television show before a live audience; and it demonstrates their talent for comedy as well as singing.

The director, Richard Lester, who had previously made two features, including *It's Trad Dad* (1962), brought to all his films a wide range of comedy techniques partly derived from television – fast cutting, jump-cutting, speeded-up action and multiple-camera set-ups – resulting in a deft lightness of touch. Filmed with the sketchiest of scripts – 'the boys go out and play in a field' reads the description of a delightful sequence in which the Beatles clown to the background of 'Can't Buy Me Love' – the movie was an immediate success, and this led to Lester's directing two further comedy hits within a year of completing *A Hard Day's Night* – *The Knack* and *Help!*

An imaginative and satirical treatment of contemporary Britain as seen by a successful writer, **Charlie Bubbles** (Memorial Enterprises/Rank, 1967) marked an appropriate and memorable debut for Albert Finney – closely associated with the 'new wave' and the break from strict realism. Somewhat bored and jaded by fame, the writer (superbly played by Finney himself in a self-effacing, low-keyed style) journeys back to his home town in the North, observing, in a detached and passive manner, the bizarre and vaguely hostile behaviour of the people he encounters. He wearily allows himself to be seduced by his scatterbrained young American secretary – Liza Minnelli in her film debut – while Billie Whitelaw and Colin Blakely perfectly fill out the parts of his tough ex-wife and wildly drunken friend; and there is a splendid performance by Timothy Garland as the writer's hostile, incommunicative young son.

A black comedy, a social satire, a sort of thriller, **Cul-de-Sac** (Compton, 1966) was the second of three feature films directed by Polish-born Roman Polanski in England during the mid-Sixties. On this picture and on *Repulsion* (1965) Polanski had the collaboration of scriptwriter Gerard Brach. *Cul-de-Sac* fulfils Polanski's expressed aim of shooting a feature that should retain the qualities of a short – simplicity, economy and unity of mood, style and setting. The entire film takes place in an extraordinary, surrealistic setting – an isolated castle on Holy Island, off the Northumberland coast, owned by an eccentric retired businessman (Donald Pleasance) who lives there with his young wife (Francoise Dorleac). The unexpected arrival of two gangsters on the run (Lionel Stander and Jack MacGowran) and the subsequent conflicts which develop between these diverse characters are in turn hilarious, pathetic and bizarre; and there are echoes of the Theatre of the Absurd, particularly Beckett and Pinter.

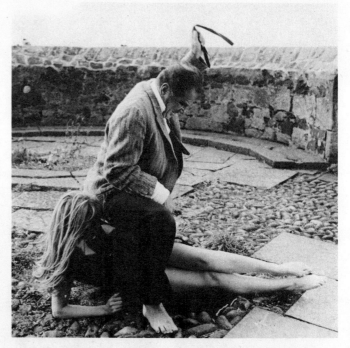

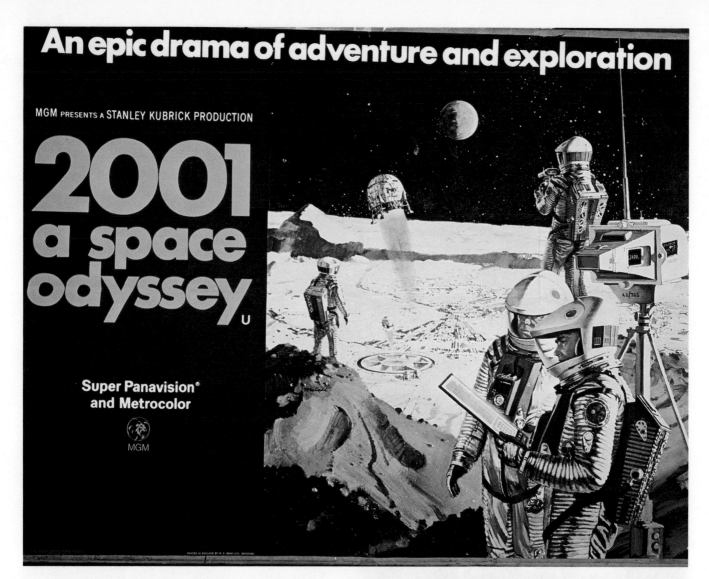

An epic drama of adventure and exploration

MGM PRESENTS A STANLEY KUBRICK PRODUCTION

2001
a space
odyssey U

Super Panavision®
and Metrocolor

MGM

SCIENCE FICTION

The future of society on earth rather than space travel has tended to be the central theme of recent science-fiction films. The trend has been evident in such diverse pictures as *Fahrenheit 451* (1966), *Planet of the Apes* (1968) and its sequels, *The President's Analyst* (1968), *Wild in the Streets* (1968), Peter Watkins's *Privilege* (1967), *The Peace Game* (1970) and *Punishment Park* (1971), *The Bed-Sitting Room* (1969), *THX 1138* (1970), *Gas!* (1970), *A Clockwork Orange* (1972) and *Sleeper* (1974). It was Kubrick, however, who, in *2001*, produced the definitive space-travel film.

The production of Stanley Kubrick's **2001: A Space Odyssey**, made by M.G.M. and released early in 1968, coincided with the preparations for the first Apollo missions to the moon. It was the product of over three years' work with the eminent science-fiction writer Arthur C. Clarke and a host of technical and special effects experts.

The picture is stunning to look at and absolutely

convincing in its simulation of modern space technology. A daringly original jump-cut from a bone thrown in the air by an ape to a spacecraft on its way to the moon (to the strains of The Blue Danube waltz) carries us forward three million years from the 'dawn of man' to the year 2001. The major portion of the film concerns the Jupiter mission undertaken by two astronauts and a computer named HAL, who emerges as the most likeable and interesting character in the film; and the final fantastic twenty minutes of this predominantly visual film (there is little plot and less dialogue) carry us into an abstract realm where 'in a moment of time too short to be measured, space turned and twisted upon itself.' In his stated intention of making a movie 'about man's relation to the universe', Kubrick was conspicuously successful.

A strange blend of science-fiction adventure, comedy and social satire, **Planet of the Apes** (Twentieth Century-Fox, 1968), adapted from Pierre Boulle's novel *Monkey Planet*, was directed by Franklin Schaffner. In the effective opening sequence a group of American astronauts crash-land on an unknown planet. After travelling through a variety of barren landscapes they reach a vast, overgrown field where they are suddenly attacked by mounted horsemen armed with deadly poles and spears. Relentlessly they are hunted down and for the first time there is a clear glimpse of the leather-jacketed, booted riders – they are apes!

Nothing in the rest of the film matches the impact of its beginning, as we follow the fortunes of a captured astronaut (Charlton Heston) held prisoner in an ape society which is a mirror image of the human world. The ape masks permit only a limited degree of characterization, while the comedy and satire, being dependent on broad effects, are lacking in subtlety. But the picture was so successful at the box office that it led to three feature-length sequels.

Kubrick's **A Clockwork Orange** (Warners, 1971) is an original and controversial picture but inferior as a piece of cinema to *Dr Strangelove* and *2001*. Adapted from the novel by Anthony Burgess, and set in a futuristic society, the film's greatest strength is the performance of Malcolm McDowell as Alex – a remarkable blend of wide-eyed innocence and perverse nastiness. The other characters are either caricatures or grotesques. Some of the settings look like slapdash studio constructions, but effective use is made of a range of 'cultural artefacts' from fibreglass nudes to womb-like chairs and thick glass tables; and Alex commits a murder with a phallic-looking piece of modern sculpture. The film may be regarded as a genuine work of 'pop art'. Its most memorable and horrifying image, however, is that of the convicted Alex being subjected to a form of Pavlovian aversion therapy, his wide eyes held forcibly open by a gruesome device clipped to his lids. Inevitably it raises the queston as to whether the violence inflicted upon Alex by the authorities is not as deplorable as that committed by him.

155

BRITISH DIRECTORS IN THE US

The transatlantic traffic in cinema talent flowed in both directions. In the late Sixties some of the most interesting American films were made by English directors – John Boorman, Peter Yates, John Schlesinger – and by Roman Polanski.

Although director John Boorman was not altogether happy about the script, adapted from Richard Stark's novel *The Hunter*, **Point Blank** (M.G.M., 1967) is an expertly made, fast-moving film, based on the theme of the individual pitted against the large, impersonal organization. Here the central character is an old-fashioned loner of a gunman (Lee Marvin) embroiled with a large-scale, corporate criminal operation behind a respectable-looking 'front'. Without delving into psychology or motivation, the picture places emphasis on action and surface appearances, superbly capturing the glossy, depersonalized feel of Los Angeles – a night-mare landscape of concrete, glass and coiling freeways. The film is notable for its violence and moments of black humour but chiefly original for its complex, episodic and dynamic structure – flashing backward and forward in time with a dazzling display of editing techniques.

Midnight Cowboy (United Artists, 1969) was adapted for the screen by veteran script-writer Waldo Salt from the novel by James Leo Herlihy and directed by John Schlesinger. A Texas greenhorn (Jon Voight) arrives in New York for the first time. Preening himself as a real 'hustler', he finds that he is the one getting 'hustled' until he teams up with a down-and-out but resilient drop-out named Ratso Rizzo (Dustin Hoffman). The initial 'country cousin meets city cousin' relationship deepens and develops into a variation of *Camille*, with Hoffman coughing his life away in the arms of his only friend. Despite some weak flashbacks and an awful moment of gratuitous violence in a seedy hotel room, the picture generally avoids sentimentality and scores with its two outstanding central performances. Hoffman completely obliterates the memory of that well-scrubbed under-graduate image created in *The Graduate*, while Voight proves almost his equal in his first major film role (both were nominated for Oscars). The picture received Oscars for best picture and best director.

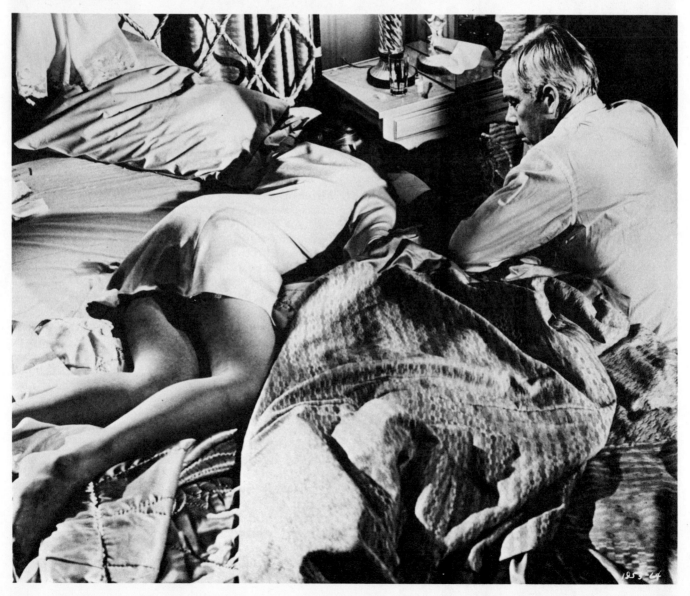

Rosemary's Baby (Paramount, 1968) was an innovation for director Roman Polanski – his first picture with a relatively large budget, his first movie shot in colour and filmed in the U.S., and his first adaptation (from the best-selling novel by Ira Levin). Here he adopts a crisp, straightforward style to convey a sharp, somewhat heightened view of the apparently normal world which is the background of the story – thus allaying our suspicions that strange things may be happening. We are kept in continual uncertainty as to whether the heroine is suffering from acute paranoia or whether she is really the victim of a devilish plot. The mannerisms of Mia Farrow are well suited to this central role as she gives the best performance of her career; and, as Polanski noted, the strength of John Cassavetes as the husband is that he does not come across as a particularly likeable character, so that we remain ignorant as to whether or not he too is involved in the plot.

Polanski's later pictures include a version of *Macbeth* (1971), filmed in Britain, an Italian black comedy, *What?* (1972), and his second American picture, *Chinatown* (1974), starring Jack Nicholson and Faye Dunaway.

British director Peter Yates was given the chance to direct **Bullitt** (1968) by Steve McQueen who had been impressed by the dramatic car chase through the streets of London featured in Yates's previous picture, *Robbery* (1967). Based on Robert Pike's novel *Mute Witness*, the character of Detective Lt. Frank Bullitt was altered to a younger, more swinging type to suit McQueen. Bullitt has the thankless task of guarding a star witness threatened by colleagues of the underworld who do not want him to testify before a Senate sub-committee on crime. Set in San Francisco, Yates brings the city to life as vividly as

Boorman does (with Los Angeles) in *Point Blank*. High point of the movie is the exciting and sometimes amusing chase through the city's hilly streets, in which McQueen did some of his own stunt driving. Since no ordinary auto could take the hills at such speeds – bouncing into the air at various points with all four wheels off the ground – it was necessary to rebuild the suspension of the cars involved. The end of the chase, when the gangsters' car catches fire and explodes, was accomplished by the last-minute substitution of a carefully guided, driverless machine.

Five years after making *Point Blank*, British director John Boorman had his second big American success with **Deliverance** (Warner Bros-Elmer enterprises, 1972). The script by James Dickey was based on his own novel about the weekend adventures of four men from the city – three relative greenhorns led by a reckless 'back to nature' enthusiast. They set out to journey by canoe down a wild Appalachian river which is soon to be destroyed by the construction of a new dam. The picture provides some pertinent comments on the erosion of the natural beauty of America by the spread of suburbia, but concentrates on a series of strange and violent encounters between the city-bred men and the local primitive, impoverished 'mountain people', underlining the gross inequalities of American society.

A particularly violent rape sequence and a couple of grisly killings ran afoul of the British censor, who tried to 'tone down' the nightmare quality of Boorman's vision, leading the latter to comment, 'I wanted to confront the audience, and the characters in the film, with the real horror of the rape and the reality of death. Not just some tomato ketchup version. He's destroyed the whole moral value of the film.'

Filmed entirely on the Chatooga River, the picture is notable for the stylized grey-green tonal range achieved by photographer Vilmos Zsigmond, who had provided the striking camerawork for Altman's *McCabe and Mrs Miller* the previous year.

SMALL BUDGET FILMS

Catering to the taste of the newly developed 'youth market' of the late Sixties were several independent and underground American film makers. And few directors mourned the departure of the Motion Picture Production Code which enabled them to treat adult themes in a more honest and explicit manner than ever before.

According to director Dennis Hopper, **Easy Rider** (Columbia, 1969) began with a phone call from Peter Fonda – 'He had an idea for a movie about two guys who smuggle cocaine, sell it, go across country for Mardi Gras and get killed by a couple of duck-hunters because they have long hair.' Hopper and Fonda then submitted the story outline to Columbia, who agreed to finance the picture on a fairly small budget. The original three-hour version, which gave 'a real feeling for the ride across country – very hypnotic, very beautiful, like in *2001*', was reduced to a more commercial 94 minutes.

The film is notable for its intelligent use of rock music – Jimi Hendrix, The Byrds, Roger McQuinn singing Dylan – and Phil Spector makes a brief but striking appearance in a hilarious pre-credits sequence. Peter Fonda may seem a bit bland as Captain America and Dennis Hopper's Billy is a real 'drag', but Jack Nicholson injects fresh life into the film with his dazzling performance as an eccentric Southern lawyer who dons a football helmet and comes along for the ride.

The picture's surprising box-office success led to a whole cycle of youth-orientated drug movies, most of which sank without a trace.

The first underground film to show at commercial cinemas, Andy Warhol's **Chelsea Girls** (1966) achieved notoriety more as a result of its outspoken dialogue, sexual byplay and drugs theme than its quality as a film. But although not as original and imaginative as some of his lesser known pictures, *Chelsea Girls* has much to recommend it. Filmed in long takes from a set position, the characters/actors relate directly to the camera and come alive on the screen with remarkable depth and authenticity, in a variety of improvised 'roles'. The film runs for three and a half hours on two screens simul-

taneously, colour reels alternating with black-and-white, so that, according to Warhol, 'you could look at one picture if you were bored with the other'. More recently Warhol's name has been associated with such pictures as *Flesh*, *Trash* and *Heat*, directed by Paul Morrissey and starring Joe d'Allesandro. *Flesh* is the most successful in blending the simpler style of early Warhol with the more conventional, commercial methods favoured by Morrissey.

Faces (Continental, 1968) which emerged from a close, four-year collaboration between director John Cassavetes and some actor-friends, extends the style of improvised film-making which he had developed in 1959–60 with a group of semi-professional actors, in making *Shadows*. The successive scenes of *Faces*, a subtly constructed

picture, resemble a series of 'set-pieces' which draw one gradually, almost imperceptibly deeper into characters and situations. A human and honest film, without heroes and villains, it reveals the diverse, even contradictory qualities to be found in any individual; and it emphasizes the 'split personality' dominating much of American society – the public image of the happy family man and successful business executive contrasting with private feelings of alienation and lack of fulfilment. The acting is superb, ranging from hilarious comedy to depths of suicidal despair. Lynn Carlin and Seymour Cassel received Oscar nominations. Working with a larger budget, Cassavetes rather disappointed expectations with *Husbands* (1969) but returned to form with *Minnie and Moskovitz* (1971), which starred Gena Rowlands and Seymour Cassel.

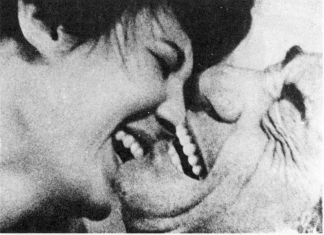

WESTERN AND GANGSTER NOSTALGIA

The mythical figures of America's past ride again – in period autos (Bonnie and Clyde) and on horseback: The Hole in the Wall Gang, also known as the Wild Bunch, which numbered among its members Butch Cassidy and the Sundance Kid – those same desperadoes who served as the inspiration for *The Great Train Robbery* in 1903.

Arthur Penn, director of **Bonnie and Clyde** (Warners/Seven Arts, 1967) had little need to embellish the extraordinary and well documented story of the criminal couple whose escapades during the early Thirties were already legendary. But by casting the attractive-looking pair of Warren Beatty and Faye Dunaway in the leading roles and deciding to shoot the film in colour, Penn deliberately stressed the romantic legend rather than the actuality, so that even the violent deaths of the couple are seen as a kind of blood-soaked ballet, in which shots are intercut from various angles and at different speeds. The realistic effect of this scene was achieved by concealing rows of explosive charges on wires under the actors' clothes (protected by padding), which were set off electrically in the correct sequence, simulating the impact of real bullets and jerking the bodies about as they exploded.

The picture was a great success critically and at the box office. All five leading players were nominated for Oscars, while Burnett Guffey was awarded an Oscar for his striking colour photography.

The Wild Bunch (Warners, 1969) is not a pretty picture. It's the story of violent people in violent times. It's a Western about the betrayal of friendship. It's about a gang of American bandits who steal a U.S. ammunition train and attempt to sell it to some Mexican revolutionaries. It's about a convict (Robert Ryan) on parole who is ordered to track down his former friends and gangmates. This is how director Sam Peckinpah described his picture. Not one to pull his punches, the opening sequence of a railroad office robbery which goes wrong is one of the most violent scenes in a violent film. Plenty of extras bite the dust, but none of the leading actors is hit, for the picture still has two hours to run; and they have to be around at the end to take on the entire Mexican army in that most famous and brutal of cinematic bloodbaths. The overall result is an uneasy blend of old-fashioned, mythic Western qualities and harsh realism, despite Peckinpah's insistence that the picture attempts to 'debunk the myth of the movie hero'. The cast includes William Holden, Ernest Borgnine and Warren Oates.

Peckinpah, an authentic Western 'character' himself, has specialized in Westerns since the early Sixties, his other pictures including *The Deadly Companions* (1961), *Guns in the Afternoon* (1962), *Major Dundee* (1965), *The Ballad of Cable Hogue* (1970), *Pat Garrett and Billy the Kid* (1973) and *Bring Me the Head of Alfredo Garcia* (1974).

A marvellously likeable and entertaining Western, **Butch Cassidy and the Sundance Kid** (Twentieth Century-Fox, 1969), directed by George Roy Hill, stresses the point that the Western outlaw has become an obvious anachronism in the twentieth century – a man who has outlived his time yet is still around to see a myth being created out of his exploits. The comedy team of Paul Newman and Robert Redford make an engaging pair of outlaws, pursuing their life of crime in a carefree, non-malicious fashion. The witty and inventive script by William Goldman is full of amusing sequences. Thus the pair end up fleeing to Bolivia with the Kid's girl (Katherine Ross), where they attempt to hold up a bank, pausing every few moments to consult a slip of paper on which are written the appropriate Spanish phrases – a moment of true slapstick comedy.

Newman, Redford and Hill teamed up again four years later for *The Sting*, which won the top Oscar in 1973.

163

CHAPTER 6

NEW DIRECTIONS

WAR

The Dirty Dozen was based on a familiar story of World War Two heroics brought up to date and made suitably violent for modern audiences; however, the best of the recent war films have attempted to extend the genre in new directions. At one extreme there is the anti-Establishment irreverence and black humour of M*A*S*H; at the other the serious, probing character study of General Patton.

Although **The Dirty Dozen** (M.G.M., 1967) was a great box-office success, there were, according to its director, Robert Aldrich, problems before work on the film began. Nunnally Johnson had written a script which Aldrich considered fine for a 1945 war picture but not for a movie made twenty years later. Lukas Heller was brought in to give it a more up-to-date feel. And if the story still seems a bit too obviously based on old-fashioned heroics, audiences clearly loved it. Much credit goes to the cast, as ugly a bunch of Hollywood 'heavies' as ever graced the screen, including Donald Sutherland, Ernie Borgnine, George Kennedy, Charles Bronson, Telly Savalas, John Cassavetes and Robert Ryan.

Led by a tough U.S. Army major (Lee Marvin) and his sergeant (Richard Jaeckel), a dozen condemned soldiers have been reprieved to carry out a dangerous mission behind enemy lines. They are subjected to a few months of rigorous training before being landed in France just prior to D-Day for a near-suicidal attack on a chateau occupied by top German officers.

Other pictures by Aldrich about World War Two have included *Attack* (1956), *The Angry Hills* (1959), *Ten Seconds to Hell* (1959) and *Too Late the Hero* (1970).

The phenomenal success of M*A*S*H (Twentieth Century-Fox, 1969) was as unexpected as that of *Easy Rider* the previous year. The script by Ring Lardner Jr. was adapted from a novel by Richard Hooker (an actual war-surgeon) for Inigo Preminger (brother of Otto) and had been turned down by a number of directors. Robert Altman agreed to do it provided he was given a free hand,

and turned the story about a mobile army hospital unit during the Korean War into a wild, anarchistic black comedy. The cast of thirty included actors who had never been in a film before and contained no obvious stars, although it created two in Elliot Gould and Donald Sutherland. As Altman admitted, 'The beauty of making M*A*S*H lay in the fact that nobody really knew what I was doing. Luckily the studio was having some large-scale problems with *Patton* and *Tora! Tora! Tora!* so we were left alone.'

The spontaneous, improvised feel of the final picture reflects the success of Altman's methods – the actors 'growing into their parts' while he continually tinkered with the script. True to form, Altman has recently parodied other traditional film genres – the Western, in *McCabe and Mrs Miller* (1971) and the private-eye movie, in *The Long Good-bye* (1973).

Patton: Lust for Glory (Twentieth Century-Fox, 1969), is based on the true story of General George Patton. Director Franklin Schaffner adhered closely to fact in tracing the general's eventful career in World War Two, but followed an essentially subjective approach, present-

ing most of the action as it might have been seen by Patton himself. George C. Scott's spirited central performance, though true to the role, pushes all other characters, from privates to generals, into the background. Indeed Patton emerges as something of a twentieth-century anachronism, his dynamic qualities more suited to a general of ancient Rome than to a commander involved in modern mass warfare; and he presents a marked contrast – as he did in reality – to those other intelligent, efficient but somewhat dull Allied generals with whom he comes in contact.

The first half of the picture deals with the campaigns in North Africa and Sicily, the friendly rivalry between Patton's tank corps and that of German General Rommel, and Patton's decisive victory at El Guettar. Relieved of his command and sent back to England for slapping a wounded soldier, Patton was then to play a key role in the liberation of France, and the climax of the second part of the film is his dramatic relief of the siege of Bastogne.

Oscars were awarded for the picture itself, to the director, to the script-writers, and to Scott in the title role.

167

THRILLERS

The growth of violence and corruption in American society was mirrored in the early Seventies by a number of intelligent, exciting thrillers and gangster pictures – evidently the most durable and popular of film styles.

The French Connection (D'Antoni/Twentieth Century-Fox, 1971) was scripted by Ernest Tidyman from the novel by Robin Moore, based on a true incident, concerning two dedicated cops on the narcotics squad (Gene Hackman and Roy Scheider) who attempt to track down 60 kilos of pure heroin smuggled into the U.S. from Marseilles. The camera, with documentary fidelity, follows the two 'narcs' through the streets, bars and nightclubs of New York. In an opening fast-action sequence they raid a seedy bar and beat up a black pusher. But when they casually drop in to a plush club they scent something bigger in the air, and this leads them on a tedious round of tailing suspects and listening to bugged conversations. An attempt on Hackman's life results in a wild race between a car and an elevated train (recalling the chase in *Bullitt*), culminating in some rather gratuitous violence before the criminal is caught. Unfortunately, director William Friedkin abandons realism in the final reels in favour of a traditional shoot-out between police and gangsters who have assembled to complete their big heroin deal.

A great success at the box office, the picture won the top Oscar, while additional awards went to director, script-writer and editor, and to Hackman for his excellent performance.

After twenty years of ups and downs as a director, Don Siegel achieved his biggest box-office success with **Dirty Harry** (Warners, 1971), the story of a police inspector (Clint Eastwood) with a dedication for hunting criminals that often takes him outside the law. An 'avenger' figure, noted for his daring feats, he interrupts his lunch at one point to foil an armed robbery single-handed; and at the climax of the picture he leaps from a railroad bridge onto the roof of a moving bus to thwart the hijack attempt of a psychotic killer (a dangerous stunt accomplished by Eastwood without using a stand-in).

Although Siegel remained 'type-cast' as a director of thrillers, he brought some variety to the genre. *Charley Varrick* (1972) was an engagingly off-beat and amusing thriller with Walter Matthau in the unlikely role of a shrewd bank robber; and *The Black Windmill* (1974), starring Michael Caine, was set in England.

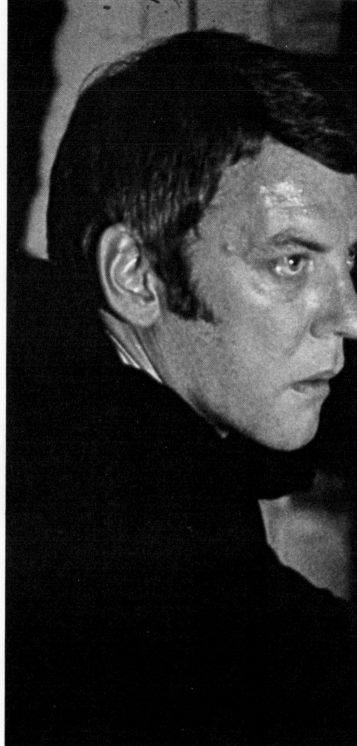

The story of **The Godfather** (Paramount, 1972) began when Paramount were offered an original script by Mario Puzo and suggested that he first turn it into a novel. The book was a best-seller and Paramount gave the project to a little-known producer (Al Ruddy), signing Francis Ford Coppola as the director. In his further work on the script, Coppola insisted on retaining the period setting and on casting actors who seemed absolutely right for the parts, despite the fact that they were either relatively unknown – such as Al Pacino, James Caan and Robert Duvall – or out of favour with Hollywood – Marlon Brando and Sterling Hayden.

The picture presents an inside view of the powerful Mafia 'families' controlling organized crime in many parts of the U.S., but concentrates upon presenting sympathetic and believable portraits of the characters, interspersing domestic events with sequences of violent action as the conflicts between rival 'families' erupt into killings and counter-killings. Although set in the Forties, the film clearly provides a comment on the violence and corruption in American society still prevailing twenty and thirty years later. Opposition to the film by various pressure groups evaporated after the producer agreed with Mafia boss Joe Columbo to delete the words 'Mafia' and 'Cosa Nostra' from the script and to use some of his 'friends' as extras.

Brando's performance in the title role as the elderly Don Corleone won him his first Oscar since *On the Waterfront* eighteen years earlier. And the enormous success of the picture led to a sequel, *Godfather part II* (1975), also directed by Coppola.

Klute (Warners, 1971) differed somewhat from the typical thriller. Although entirely contemporary in subject and treatment, the picture handled sex and violence with remarkable discretion, placing its main emphasis on characters and relationships. As director Alan Pakula pointed out, 'You see very little violence in *Klute*. You hear murder. You don't see it. And partly that's because

I'm much more interested in the actual terror, in the danger. . . . There is also comparatively little actual sexual activity. There *are* a lot of words, for a particular reason. It was the story of a girl obsessed with the need to 'seduce' men. She was almost destroyed by that compulsion. And the words were part of her siren call.' Jane Fonda's convincing performance as the call-girl, Bree Daniels, won her an Oscar; and Donald Sutherland was excellent in the less demanding role of Klute, the detective whose search for a missing man involves him with Bree. Filmed on location in New York, the movie admirably captures the strange and sordid world inhabited by Bree and her friends.

ANIMATED FEATURES

Feature-length animated films produced in the late Sixties and early Seventies, were represented at one extreme by the reliable family entertainment of the Disney Studios and at the other by the films of Ralph Bakshi and Steve Krantz; and the one notable British achievement in this field was *The Yellow Submarine*.

The Yellow Submarine (Apple/King Features/United Artists, 1968) stemmed from a Beatles cartoon series produced in London late in 1965 by TV Cartoons under the supervision of George Dunning. The idea for the picture was first developed by producer Al Brodax and director Dunning, and after some trial animation the project took on a new lease of life when German graphic artist Heinz Edelmann joined the team as chief designer. The story tells of the invasion of Pepperland by the evil Blue Meanies, who are eventually routed by Old Fred, conductor of Sergeant Pepper's Lonely Hearts Club Band, and the Beatles in the Yellow Submarine. An inventive set of characters include the Vacuum Flask Monster, Ferocious Flying Glove, Nowhere Man and Butterfly Stompers; and the music, is of course, provided by the Beatles. The result is a delightful and memorable film – a compilation of modern graphic styles from Pop to Op, art nouveau to surrealism, psychedelics to Freudian symbolism.

The most delightful full-length animated cartoon produced by the Disney Studios during the Sixties, **The Jungle Book** (Disney, 1967), inspired by the stories of Rudyard Kipling, was the last picture supervised by Disney himself, who died in 1966. The story of Mowgli, the boy raised in the jungle by a pair of wolves, presented an excellent opportunity for a variety of visual effects – shadows, reflections, moonlight, etc. And the characterization of the jungle animals was achieved by combining the clever visuals with the delightfully appropriate voices of George Sanders, Phil Harris, Louis Prima and Sebastian Cabot.

Easy-going and unpretentious, the picture was one of several feature-length Disney cartoons to appear during the Sixties, including *101 Dalmatians* (1961), *The Sword in the Stone* (1963), *Winnie the Pooh and the Honey Tree* (1966) and *The Aristocats* (1969).

Fritz the Cat (Fritz productions/Fox-Rank, 1971), based on an underground comic strip by Robert Crumb, was the first attempt by producer Steve Krantz and writer-director Ralph Bakshi to make a truly adult, feature-length cartoon, a kind of 'antidote' to Disney. The picture stands up in its own right as an imaginative satire on the typical white liberal college drop-out of the Sixties, with cops portrayed as pigs, blacks represented by crows, and so forth. The striking opening sequence shows Fritz in Washington Square picking up a she-cat and two of her girl friends and inviting them back to his East Village pad. One of Bakshi's innovations was to use photographs of actual New York settings as the basis for

stylized backgrounds, while part of the soundtrack was constructed from cinema-vérité-style tape recordings of real conversations. An outstanding rock and jazz soundtrack includes contributions by B. B. King, Bo Diddley and Billie Holliday.

Although the picture cost $1 million, it was a big commercial success; but later cartoons from producer Krantz – *Heavy Traffic* (1973), directed by Bakshi, and *The Nine Lives of Fritz the Cat* (1974), directed by Robert Taylor – failed to match up to the first *Fritz*.

PERMISSIVE CINEMA

A variety of recent pictures dealing with aspects of the American scene, ranging from *The Last Picture Show* to *The Exorcist*, and *Who's Afraid of Virginia Woolf?* to *The Last Detail*, reflect the work of new young directors, among them Peter Bogdanovich, William Friedkin, Mike Nichols and Hal Ashby.

For Mike Nichols **The Graduate** (Embassy, 1967) marked a distinct contrast in style and subject to *Who's Afraid of Virginia Woolf?*, just as his third film, *Catch-22* (1970) represented yet another departure for this most chameleon-like of directors. The central character of this enjoyable and entertaining picture is a recent college graduate (Dustin Hoffman in his first role) who is trapped into an affair with Mrs Robinson (Anne Bancroft) and then finds himself falling in love with her teenage daughter (Katherine Ross). Aside from the fine performances of Hoffman and Bancroft, the picture's best moments are in those opening sequences which satirize the high-powered, glossy, superficial world of Southern Californian society. Nichols's free and easy style of direction won him an Oscar, while the delightful soundtrack, supplied by Simon and Garfunkel, included a number of songs specially written for the picture.

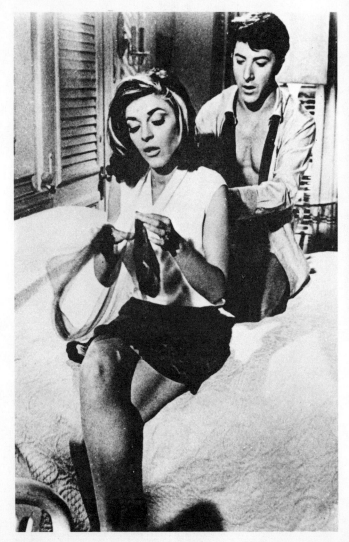

Mike Nichols's film version of **Who's Afraid of Virginia Woolf?** (Warners, 1966) retained much of the intimacy and concentration of Edward Albee's play which Nichols had previously directed on Broadway, events taking place in the course of a single night and most of the action being confined to one house. Much of the original outspoken dialogue was also kept in, though slightly toned down.

The stormy marriage between Martha and George and the ferocity of their intense love-hate relationship is revealed through their 'fun and games' with a younger couple invited over for drinks one night. All four players in the cast give riveting performances, particularly Elizabeth Taylor, here discarding her glamorous image and adding some years to her true age as the shrewish wife of the second-rate college lecturer, played by Richard Burton. She won an Oscar for what was perhaps the finest performance of her career, Sandy Dennis won the supporting Oscar, while Burton and George Segal received nominations. Haskell Wexler won the last Oscar for black-and-white photography, this award being discontinued now that most pictures were colour.

The Last Picture Show (BBS/Columbia, 1971) was the first of three pictures in which director Peter Bogdanovich, tapping a nostalgic streak of unexpected dimensions in the film-going public, achieved spectacular success. The picture recreates the world of a small-town Texas community of the early Fifties, and the theme reflected in the film's title is the declining popularity of the last remaining local movie theatre. The plot is concerned with the experiences of a cross-section of townspeople, particularly three high-school students in their final year (played by screen newcomers Jeff Bridges, Cybill Shepherd and Timothy Bottoms). If the human interest balance and sexual intrigue veer a little too close to Peyton Place, there is no denying the sensitivity with which the milieu is brought to life on the screen, nor the high standard of the acting (Cloris Leachman and Ben Johnson won Oscars for their supporting roles).

The film grossed well over $15 million, as did Bogdanovich's two subsequent pictures, *What's Up Doc?* (1972), a homage to Thirties screwball comedy, and *Paper Moon* (1973), also set in the Thirties.

Extraordinary and bizarre, vulgar and revealing, the performance of Marlon Brando completely dominates **Last Tango in Paris** (Grimaldi/United Artists, 1972) to such an extent that most of the plot, subplot and minor characters fade into the background. Maria Schneider, his co-star, does well for an inexperienced actress, but her role is essentially passive, little more than that of a sex object who feeds and stimulates Brando's fantasies. The story, about a man and a girl in a vacant Paris apartment where they indulge in a variety of sexual and emotional games, was originally meant to star Jean Louis Trintignant and Dominique Sanda, featured in the previous picture by director Bernardo Bertolucci, *The Conformist* (1970). Although the original framework was retained Brando's presence transformed the picture.

Bertolucci gave Brando a great deal of freedom, allowing him partially to improvise his role; and drawing heavily on his own background and experience, Brando opened up as few actors had done before. His performance has a roughness and brutal power which appears both honest and uncontrived, making the eccentric sexual behaviour and filthy language seem entirely acceptable. The question is – after *The Godfather* and *Last Tango*, where is there for Brando to go?

The controversy surrounding **The Exorcist** (Warners, 1973) makes it a difficult picture to assess on its merits. It was scripted by William Peter Blatty from his own best-selling novel (loosely derived from a true case history) and directed by William Friedkin. The story of a young girl apparently possessed by the devil is treated with intelligence and imagination and contains many moments of outrageous black humour. The sensational newspaper headlines, concentrating on particular sequences and raising irrelevant ethical issues, aroused the wrath of would-be censors out of all proportion to what is actually seen and experienced in the film itself. The picture is, in fact, an entertaining and accomplished piece of cinema, especially memorable for its sound effects which, with Blatty's screenplay, won an Oscar. The acting, too, is excellent, especially that of Jason Miller as the young, dedicated priest, Ellen Burstyn as the distraught mother and Linda Blair as the possessed Regan.

Based on a novel by Darryl Ponicsan, **The Last Detail** (Columbia-Warner, 1974) tells the story of a pair of Petty Officers and a young recruit, sentenced to eight years in the brig for the attempted theft of $40, whom they are escorting from the naval base in Norfolk, Virginia to Portsmouth Naval Prison in New Hampshire. The two older men develop a liking for their inexperienced charge – a tall, gangly young man seemingly indifferent to his fate, accustomed to being pushed around and full of self-destructive impulses – and try to introduce him to some of the pleasures offered by the cities en route (Washington, New York and Boston). Filmed entirely on location, the film conveys an accurate impression of the winter journey northward and the ending, as the prison gates clang shut behind the sentenced man, is characteristically bleak.

Jack Nicholson gives a suitably down-to-earth performance as 'Bad-Ass' Buddusky, the tough, outspoken leader of the threesome. Coupled with his playing of Thirties private-eye J. J. Gittes in Polanski's *Chinatown* (1974), this role further confirms Nicholson's claim to be regarded as the top American film actor of the Seventies. For Hal Ashby this is his third and best feature as a director, previous films being *The Landlord* (1970) and the delightful black comedy *Harold and Maud* (1971). All three pictures present a critical, good-natured view of the contemporary American scene.

Love Story (Minsky/Hiller/Paramount, 1970) was based on a story by Erich Segal which was simultaneously turned into a novel, the book becoming a best-seller while the film was drawing crowds at the box office. The story of the tragic romance between a hockey-playing Harvard undergraduate from a well-to-do family and an attractive music student from Radcliffe made stars of comparative newcomers Ryan O'Neal and Ali MacGraw; and Ray Milland makes a brief but effective appearance as Ryan's millionaire father. A well-made but uninspiring piece of cinema, the picture's commercial success provoked widespread attacks from the critics, although it is hard to understand what all the fuss was about. The film was directed by Arthur Hiller whose most notable picture of the Sixties was a rather unusual anti-war satire, *The*

Americanization of Emily (1964), based on a script by Paddy Chayefsky and starring Julie Andrews.

NEW BRITISH DIRECTORS

Making their mark on the British film scene during the late Sixties were new directors such as Ken Loach and Ken Russell, who had gained their previous experience in television, and Nicolas Roeg, who had been a top cameraman before he graduated to directing.

Ken Russell first made his name as a film director with the highly successful **Women in Love** (United Artists, 1969), adapted from the novel by D. H. Lawrence. The turn-of-the-century setting and artistic milieu were already familiar to him through his celebrated television films on the lives of Elgar, Debussy, Delius and Isadora Duncan, and he recognized the story as the most challenging opportunity of his career thus far – '. . . to dig into the shifting reassessments of relationships and their ever-changing surfaces, while nature, too, plays a great part in the story. Lawrence's feelings for the country were so immense, so physical, that the visual effect needs to be tactile in its impact.' Inevitably, Russell was obliged to concentrate on externals of character, places and events, but succeeded admirably in capturing the feel of Edwardian England – the country landscapes and garden parties, the dirt and squalor of a mining town and the contrasting luxury of the mine owners' homes.

The acting is of a high standard, especially that of Alan Bates in Lawrence's semi-autobiographical role of Rupert Birkin, and of Glenda Jackson as Gudrun – a performance which earned her an Oscar.

Russell has emerged during the Seventies as the most prolific and talented, if somewhat undisciplined, of British directors, with six additional features that include *The Music Lovers* (1970), *The Devils* (1971) and *Mahler* (1974).

Kes (United Artists, 1969) was the first feature film of producer Tony Garnett and director Ken Loach who had been responsible for a number of outstanding and controversial B.B.C. television plays, including *Cathy Come Home*, *Up the Junction* and *In Two Minds*. Separating briefly in 1967, when Loach directed his first feature, *Poor Cow*, they were reunited under the banner of Kestrel Film Productions for *Kes* and for *Family Life* (1971), based on David Mercer's *In Two Minds*.

Kes, based on the novel *Kestrel for a Knave* by Barry Hines, is the story of a rebellious teenager who devotes himself to training a young kestrel, thus revealing his true intelligence and potential in life which is clearly going to waste. Loach stresses the parallel between boy and bird – he will be forced into the system as a manual worker by his need to earn money just as the training of the kestrel is based on its need for food. Barnsley schoolboy David Bradley, who has subsequently won fame (as Dai Bradley) on the London stage, was actually taught how to train a fledgling kestrel in front of the cameras. Filmed entirely on location in Yorkshire, *Kes* is a fascinating and stirring picture as well as a valuable 'social document'.

An original and extraordinary work, **Performance** (Warners, 1969) so baffled its distributors and alienated the censor that it was shelved for two years before being released. The film was the result of a close collaboration of friends – producer Sandy Lieberson, writer Donald Cammell and photographer Nicolas Roeg, with Cammell and Roeg co-directing. Mick Jagger, in his first film part, as an ex-rock star, contributed to the fantasy world created around his character and provided the hit song 'Memo from Turner'; and James Fox gave a remarkable portrayal of the strong-arm man, or 'performer', on the run both from the police and his fellow gangsters. The atmosphere of the South London underworld was brought authentically to life in the first half of the picture, and it was the violence of certain sequences which so outraged the censor and led to a number of long cuts.

Nicholas Roeg's more recent films as a director include *Walkabout* (1970) and *Don't Look Now* (1973).

One of the most durable of film 'properties', **The Three Musketeers** (Fox-Rank) was most recently filmed in Spain in 1973 by director Richard Lester and released in two parts – *The Queen's Diamonds* (1974) and *The Four Musketeers* (1975). While remaining faithful to the spirit of the Dumas book full of romance and swashbuckling action, Lester subtly undercut the heroics by introducing a strong note of realism and some fine moments of slapstick comedy. Acrobatic stunts frequently go awry, swordsmen expend a great deal of fruitless energy, and the rich assortment of background detail continually draws attention to the fact that the general tone of life at that time was nasty, squalid and distinctly unromantic. Michael York makes an appropriately willing and eager D'Artagnan, with Oliver Reed, Frank Finlay and Richard Chamberlain as the three contrasting musketeers.

Prelim and Chapter opening pictures not identified elsewhere:
Front endpapers The Three Musketeers
Back endpapers The Wild Bunch
Pages 4–5 Forty-Second Street
Page 6 Elizabeth Taylor in Cleopatra
Page 8 Dustin Hoffman in Lenny
Page 10 Ramon Novarro and May McAvoy in Ben Hur
Page 11 A Dog's Life
Page 63 Humphrey Bogart in The Big Sleep
Page 132 Marilyn Monroe and Clark Gable in The Misfits
Page 133 Steve McQueen in Bullitt
Page 164 Gene Hackman in The French Connection
Page 165 Marlon Brando in The Godfather

INDEX AND ACKNOWLEDGMENTS

A Nous La Liberté 46
Accident 152
Across the Pacific 95
Adam's Rib 92, 93, 94
Admirable Crichton, The 16
Adventures of Robin Hood, The 48, *48*, 49
Advise and Consent 148
African Queen, The 95, *95*
Agee, James 23, 95
Air Force 76
Alamo, The 134
Aldrich, Robert 117, 166
All About Eve 94, 96, 98, *98*
All the King's Men 86, 88, *89*, 148
All Quiet on the Western Front 24, 30, *30*, 77
Allen, Woody 72
Allied Artists 146
Altman, Robert 158, 166
Ambler, Eric 74
American in Paris, An 43, 115
Americanization of Emily, The 183
Anatahan 35
Anatomy of a Murder 117, *117*
Anderson, Judith 79, 126
Anderson, Lindsay 74, 141, 150
Anderson, Maxwell 126
Andress, Ursula 138
Andrews, Dana 76, 77, *77*, 79
Andrews, Julie 143, 144, 183
Angel Face 79
Angry Hills, The 166
Animal Crackers 46
Animal Farm 109, *110*
Anna Karenina 54
Antonioni, Michelangelo 150
Apache 101
Apartment, The 137, *137*
Applause 27
Aristocats, The 172
Arnold, Elliott 101
Around the World in Eighty Days 126, 128, *128*
Arthur, Jean 56, 103
As You Like It 74
Ashby, Hal 176, 180
Asphalt Jungle, The 97, *97*, 136
Asquith, Anthony 52, 73
Astaire, Fred 38, *42*, 43, 115

Astor, Mary 48
Attack 166
Avanti 136
Avedon, Richard 115
Axelrod, George 115
Ayres, Lew 30

Baby Face Nelson 119, *121*
Bacall, Lauren 79
Bad and the Beautiful, The 96, *98*, 98
Baker, Stanley 109
Bakshi, Ralph 172, 174
Balderston, John 48
Ballad of Cable Hogue, The 162
Bambi 61
Bancroft, Anne 176
Band Wagon, The 30
Bank Dick, The 48, *48*
Barrault, Jean-Louis 32
Barrie, J. M. 16
Barrymore, Diana 98
Barrymore, John 27, 32, 37, 98
Barrymore, Lionel *36*, 37, 54, 86
Bart, Lionel 143, 144
Batchelor, Joy 104, 109
Bates, Alan 184
Baum, Frank 52
Baxter, Warner 30, *31*
Beatles 152, *153*, 172
Beaton, Cecil 115
Beatty, Warren 162
Beckett, Samuel 152
Bed-Sitting Room, The 154
Beery, Wallace *36*, 37
Behrman, S. N. 126
Bel Geddes, Barbara 97
Bellamy, Ralph 67
Belle of the Nineties 35
Ben Hur (1923–5) *10*, *15*, 16
Ben Hur (1958), 126, *126*
Bennett, Joan 56
Benny, Jack 69
Benson, Sally 68
Bergner, Elizabeth 74
Bergman, Ingrid 72, *73*, 78, 130
Berkeley, Busby 30, 31, 54
Berkeleys of Broadway 29
Berlin, Irving 43
Bernstein, Leonard 93, 103
Bertolucci, Bernardo 179
Best Man, The 148
Best Years of Our Lives, The 76, 77
Bezzerides, A. I. 117

Big Country, The 85
Big Heat, The 116, 117
Big Knife, The 96
Big Parade, The 24, *24*, 86
Big Sleep, The 79, *79*
Birds, The 130
Birth of a Nation, The 12, 13, 56, 86
Black Windmill, The 168
Blackboard Jungle, The 119
Blackmail 27, *27*
Blair, Linda 180
Blakely, Colin 152
Blatty, William Peter 180
Bloom, Claire 109
Blore, Eric 43, 69
Blow-up 150, *150*
Blue Angel, The 26, 27
Body and Soul 88
Boehm, Sidney 117
Bogarde, Dirk 152
Bogart, Humphrey *63*, 72, 79, *79*, 95, *95*, 97, 117
Bogdanovich, Peter 176, 179
Bolger, Ray 52
Bolt, Robert 134
Bond, Ward 124
Bonnie and Clyde 162, *162*
Boomerang 88
Boorman, John 156, 158
Borgnine, Ernest 162, 166
Born Yesterday 88, *92*, 93
Bottoms, Timothy 179
Boulle, Pierre 128, 155
Bow, Clara 27
Boy Friend, The 30
Boyd, Stephen 126
Boyer, Charles 128
Brabin, Charles 16
Bracken, Eddie 68
Bradley, David (Dai) 184, *184*
Brando, Marlon 103, *103*, 105, 112, 170, 171, 179, *179*
Brennan, Walter 122, 125
Brice, Fanny 144
Bride of Frankenstein, The 37, *37*
Bridge on the River Kwai, The 80, 126, 128, 134
Bridges, Jeff 179
Brief Encounter 74, 80, *80*, 81
Bring Me the Head of Alfredo Garcia 162
British Lion 74, 85, 106
Brodax, Al 172
Broderick, Helen 43

Broken Arrow 101, *101*
Bronson, Charles 166
Browning Version, The 52
Bruce, Virginia 54
Brynner, Yul 126
Burke, Billy 36
Burstyn, Ellen 180
Burton, Richard 135, 177
Butch Cassidy and the Sundance Kid 163, *163*

Caan, James 170
Cabaret 146, *146–7*
Cabiria 12
Cabot, Sebastian 172
Cagney, James 32, 41
Caine, Michael 168
Calhern, Louis 98
Call Northside 777 86, 88, *88*
Camille 28, *52*, 54, *55*, 156
Cammell, Donald 184
Cantinflas 128
Capra, Frank 23, 30, 41
Carey, Joyce 80
Carlin, Lynn 161
Caron, Leslie 115
Carousel 144
Carradine, John *44*, 65, 126
Carroll, Madeleine 48
Casablanca 72, *72*
Cassavetes, John 158, 160, 166
Cassel, Seymour 161
Catch 22 176
Chamberlain, Richard 187
Chandler, Jeff 101
Chandler, Raymond 79
Chaney, Lon Jr 65
Chaplin, Charlie *11*, 16, 18, 22, *22*, 24, 46, *46*, 69, 86
Charge of the Light Brigade, The 138
Charisse, Cyd 95, 115
Charley Varrick 168
Charlie Bubbles 152, *153*
Chase, Borden 86
Chayefsky, Paddy 183
Cheat, The 16
Chelsea Girls 160
Chevalier, Maurice 31, *31*
Cheyenne Autumn 122
Chinatown 158, 180
Chump at Oxford, A 46–7, *47*
Churchill, Berton 44
Cincinnati Kid, The 148
Cinemascope 119, 148

Citadel, The 38
Citizen Kane 65, 70, 71, 77, 88
City Lights 46
City Streets 31
Clair, René 46
Clarens, Carlos 37
Clarke, Arthur C. 154
Clarke, Mae 32
Clayton, Jack 141
Cleopatra (1934) 16
Cleopatra (1963) 6, 16, 134–5, *135*, 144
Clift, Montgomery 86, 103, 136
Clockwork Orange, A 150, 154, 155, *155*
Cobb, Lee J. 103
Cocoanuts 27, 46
Cohn, Harry 88, 94
Colbert, Claudette 41, 98
Collins, Joan 134
Colman, Ronald 48, 128
Columbia Pictures 30, 39, 41, 43, 67, 88, 93, 94, 103, 117, 124, 128, 135, 144, 148, 160, 179
Columbia-Warner 180
Comden and Green 93, 94
Compulsion 119
Confidential Report 88
Conformist, The 179
Connery, Sean 138
Conquest of Space 122
Cook, Elisha Jr 103, 120
Cooper, Gary 27, 31, 72, *73*, 101
Cooper, Merian C. 41
Coppola, Francis Ford 170, 171
Corman, Roger 150
Corsia, Ted de 120
Cortazar, Julio 150
Cotten, Joseph 86
Countess from Hong Kong, The 86
Cover Girl 30, 93
Coward, Noël 73, 74, 80
Craig, Wendy 152
Crawford, Broderick 88, 93
Crawford, Joan 23, 37
Crimson Kimono, The 119
Crisp, Donald 66
Cromwell, John 48
Crowd, The 24
Crumb, Robert 172
Cry of the City 88
Cukor, George 37, 54, 56, 93, 112, 143
Cul-de-Sac 150, 152, *152*

Cure, The 18
Currie, Finlay 81
Curse of Frankenstein, The 108
Curtis, Ken 124
Curtis, Tony 137
Curtiz, Michael 48, 66, 72
Cushing, Peter 108

Daddy Long Legs 115
Dalio, Marcel 72
D'Allesandro, Joe 160
Dames 31
Daniels, William 37, 54
Darwell, Jane 65, 65
Dassin, Jules 88
Daves, Delmer 101, 122, 125
Davis, Bette 94, 98, 98
Dawn Patrol, The 27
Deadly Companions, The 162
Dean, James 91, 119
Delaney, Shelagh 141
Deliverance 158, 159
Demarest, William 69
Demi-Paradise, The 74
DeMille, Cecil B. 16, 98, 126
Dennis, Sandy 177
Destry Rides Again 122
Devil is a Woman, The 35
Devil Rides Out, The 109
Devils, The 184
Devine, Andy 44
Diamond Lil 35
Diary for Timothy, A 73
Dickens, Charles 81, 144
Dickey, James 158
Dickinson, Angie 125
Dickinson, Thorold 80, 82
Dietrich, Marlene 26, 27, 30, 34, 35, 128
Dillon, Carmen 74
DiMaggio, Joe 115
Dinner at Eight 36, 37
Dirty Dozen, The 166
Dirty Harry 168
Dishonoured 35
Disney, Walt 59–61
Disney Studios 142, 172
Dix, Richard 16
Dodge City 48
Dog's Life, A 11, 18, 18
Don Juan 27
Donat, Robert 38, 50
Donen, Stanley 93, 94, 115
Don't Look Now 184
Dorleac, Françoise 152
Double Indemnity 78
Douglas, Kirk 98
Dr Doolittle 144
Dr Jekyll and Mr Hyde 32, 32
Dr No 138, 139
Dr Strangelove 148, 149, 155
Dr Zhivago 80
Dracula 108
Drisse, Gus 82
Drum, The 50
Drums Along the Mohawk 85
Duck Soup 46
Duel in the Sun 24, 85–6, 86
Dumbo 61
Dumont, Margaret 47
Dunaway, Faye 158, 162, 187
Duncan, Isadora 183
Dunning, George 172
Duvall, Robert 170

Eagle-Lion 74
Ealing Films 80, 83, 104, 108
Earthquake 59
Easdale, Brian 83
East of Eden 119
Eastman Colour 109

Eastwood, Clint 168, 169
Easy Rider 160, 160–1, 166
Easy Street 18
Edelmann, Heinz 172
Edens, Roger 93
Edison Company 12
Eisner, Lotte 21
El Cid 134
El Dorado 122, 125
Elam, Jack 120
Elephant Boy 50, 50
Elmer Enterprises 158
Embassy Films 176
Emerson, John 59
Entertainer, The 141
Evergreen 38, 39
Ewell, Tom 114, 115
Exodus 134, 135, 135
Exorcist, The 176, 180, 180

Faces 160, 161
Fahrenheit 451, 154
Fail Safe 148
Fairbanks, Douglas Jr 48
Fairbanks, Douglas Sr 14, 15, 16, 48, 51, 59
Falcon Films 81
Fall of the Roman Empire 134
Fallen Angel 79
Fallen Idol, The 85, 144
Family Life 184
Famous Players-Lasky 16, 27
Fantasia 61, 61
Far Country, The 122, 123
Farewell to Arms, A 72
Farmer's Wife, The 27
Farnum, Franklyn 98
Farrow, Mia 158
Fernandel 128
Fiddlers Three 80
Field, Bette 65
Fields, W. C. 46, 47–8, 48
Fifty-five Days at Peking 134
Finlay, Frank 187
Finlayson, James 47
Finney, Albert 138, 138, 141, 152
Fires Were Started 73, 73
First of the Few, The 52, 74
First a Girl 38
First National 18, 23
Fisher, Terence 108, 109
Fitzgerald, Barry 106
Flaherty, Robert 19, 50
Fleming, Victor 52, 56
Flesh 160
Flower Drum Song 144
Flowers and Trees 59
Flying Down to Rio 43
Fonda, Henry 65, 65, 85, 117
Fonda, Jane 120, 171
Fonda, Peter 160
Foolish Wives 19, 19
Footlight Parade 31
For Whom the Bell Tolls 72, 73
Forbes, Bryan 148
Forbidden Planet 120, 120
Ford, Glenn 117, 124
Ford, John 20, 20, 21, 43, 44, 65, 66, 85, 104, 106, 122
Foreman, Carl 101
Fortune Cookie, The 137
49th Parallel, The 74
Forty-Second Street 4–5, 30
Fosse, Bob 146
Four Devils, The 21
Four Horsemen of the Apocalypse, The 24, 25
Fox Films 20, 21, 43, 65, 66, 76, 79, 85, 88, 96, 98, 101, 112, 115, 119, 134, 144, 148, 155, 163, 166, 168, 187

Fox, James 152, 184
Fox, Julian 27
Francis, Anne 120
Frankenheimer, John 148
Frankenstein, John 148
Frankenstein 37
Free Cinema movement 141, 150
French CanCan 104
French Connection, The 168, 168
Frenzy 130
Friedkin, William 168, 176, 180
Fritz the Cat 172, 174, 174
Front Page, The 67, 136
Fuller, Sam 119
Funny Face 43, 112, 115, 115
Funny Girl 144, 146
Funny Thing Happened on the Way to the Forum, A 187
Furse, Roger 74, 109
Fury 117

Gable, Clark 41, 52, 56, 57, 58, 59, 132, 137
Garbo, Greta 28, 54
Garfield, John 88, 97
Garland, Judy 52, 53, 68, 112
Garland, Timothy 152
Garmes, Lee 35
Garnett, Tony 184
Gas! 154
Gaumont-British 38, 50
Gay Divorcee, The 43
Gaynor, Janet 21, 44, 45, 112
Gazzara, Ben 117
General, The 22, 23
General Died at Dawn, The 76
Gentleman's Agreement 96
Gentlemen Prefer Blondes 90, 112, 113, 115
Gershwin, George and Ira 115
Giant 85, 103, 119
Gibbons, Cedric 37
Gielgud, John 103, 109
Gilbert, John 20, 24
Girl Can't Help It, The 112
Gish, Lillian 86
Gleason, Jackie 148
Glenn Miller Story, The 122
Gloag, Julian 141
Go-Between, The 152
Go West Young Man 35
Godard, Jean-Luc 150
Goddard, Paulette 46, 56
Godfather, The 170, 170, 179
Godfather II 171
Gold Diggers of 1933 31
Gold Rush, The 22, 22
Golden Coach, The 104
Goldmann, William 163
Goldwyn, Sam 16, 20, 66, 77
Golem, The 27
Gone With the Wind 52, 56, 56, 57, 86, 144
Good Companions, The 38
Good Earth, The 52
Gordon, Leo 120
Gordon, Ruth 93
Goring, Marius 82
Gough-Yates, Kevin 76
Gould, Elliot 166
Gowland, Gibson 20
Graduate, The 156, 176, 176
Grand Hotel 37
Grant, Cary 35, 35, 67, 67, 79, 130, 131
Grapes of Wrath, The 62, 65, 65, 66, 85
Gray, Joel 146
Great Dictator, The 46, 69

Great Expectations 81, 81
Great Gatsby, The 141
Great Moment, The 68
Great Train Robbery, The 11, 11, 162
Great Ziegfeld, The 37, 52, 54, 54, 59
Greed 20
Green, Guy 81
Greenwood, Joan 83
Griffith, D. W. 12, 13, 16, 24, 56, 86
Griffith, Hugh 126
Guffey, Burnett 162
Guinness, Sir Alec 81, 83, 108, 128, 129, 134
Guns in the Afternoon 122, 162
Guns of Naverone, The 134
Guys and Dolls 103, 112

Hackman, Gene 164, 168, 168
Hagen, Jean 95
Hail the Conquering Hero 68, 68
Halas, John 104, 109
Hale, Alan 48
Haley, Jack 52, 53
Hallelujah! 24
Halls of Montezuma, The 77
Hamilton, Margaret 52
Hamlet 81, 109
Hammer Films 104, 108
Hammerstein, Oscar 144
Harburg, E. Y. 52
Hard Day's Night, A 150, 152, 153
Hardwicke, Cedric 109, 126
Hardy, Oliver 46
Harlow, Jean 32, 36, 37
Harold and Maude 181
Harris, Phil 172
Harris, Richard 141
Harrison, Rex 135, 143
Harvey, Laurence 141, 148
Haskins, Byron 122
Hathaway, Henry 88
Havilland, Olivia de 48, 56
Hawkins, Jack 134
Hawks, Howard 39, 66, 67, 78, 79, 85, 86, 112, 122, 125
Hayakawa, Sessue 128
Haycox, Ernest 44
Hayden, Sterling 97, 170
Hayward, Susan 56, 134
Hayworth, Rita 88
Hearts of the World 24
Heavy Traffic 174
Hecht, Ben 66, 67, 78
Heckroth, Hein 83, 106
Heflin, Van 102, 103, 124
Heller, Lukas 166
Heller, Otto 82
Heller in Pink Tights 112
Hello Dolly 144, 146
Hell's Angels 27
Help! 152
Helpmann, Robert 82, 106
Hemmings, David 150, 150
Henreid, Paul 72
Henry V 74, 75, 81, 103, 109
Hepburn, Audrey 112, 115, 115, 142, 143
Hepburn, Katharine 93, 95
Hersholt, Jean 20
Heston, Charlton 126, 154, 155, 187
High Noon 100, 101, 124, 125
High Wind in Jamaica, A 108
Hill, George Roy 163
Hiller, Wendy 52, 52
Hines, Barry 184
His Girl Friday 67, 67
Hitchcock, Alfred 27, 50,

78, 79, 129–30
Hobson, Valerie 37, 81, 83
Hoffman, Dustin 7, 156, 157, 176
Hoffman, E. T. A. 106
Holden, William 94, 98, 128, 162
Holliday, Judy 93, 94
Holloway, Stanley 80
Hope, Anthony 48
Hopkins, Miriam 32
Hopper, Dennis 160
Horner, Robert 83
Horse Feathers 46
Horten, Edward Everett 43
Hound of the Baskervilles, The 109
House of Bamboo 119
House on 92nd Street, The 88
Houseman, John 71, 103
How Green Was My Valley 65, 66, 66
Howard, Leslie 52, 52, 57, 74
Howard, Sidney 56
Howard, Trevor 80
Howe, James Wong 48
Hudson, Rock 101
Hughes, Howard 39
Hunt, Martita 81
Hunter, Jeffrey 124
Husbands 161
Hustler, The 148, 148
Huston, John 78, 95, 96, 97, 136

I Am a Camera 146
I Confess 129
I Know Where I'm Going 76
I Walked with a Zombie 71, 71
I Was a Spy 38
Ibàñez, Vicente Blasco 24
If 150, 151
I'm No Angel 35
Immigrant, The 18
In Which We Serve 74, 74, 128
Informer, The 43, 43
Ingram, Rex 16, 24, 48
Inherit the Wind 119
Innocents, The 141
Intolerance 13, 16
Invasion of the Body Snatchers, The 120
Ipcress File, The 138
Irma la Douce 136
Iron Horse, The 20–1, 20, 21
Isadora 141
It Happened One Night 41, 41
It's Love Again 38
It's Trad Dad 152

Jackson, Glenda 184
Jaeckel, Richard 166
Jane Eyre 71
Jannings, Emil 27
Jarre, Maurice 134
Jazz Singer, The 27
Jennings, Humphrey 73
Johnson, Ben 179
Johnson, Celia 80
Johnson, Nunnally 166
Jones, Carolyn 120
Jones, Darby 71, 71
Jones, Jennifer 86
Journey into Fear 88
Journey's End 37
Joyless Street 27
Judgment at Nuremburg 119
Julius Caesar 103
Jungle Book, The 50, 172, 175

Kanin, Garson 93
Kantor, MacKinlay 77
Karas, Anton 85

187

Karloff, Boris 37
Kaufman, Boris 104
Kazan, Elia 88, 96, 97, 103, 104
Keaton, Buster 22, 23, 46, 98, 128
Keeler, Ruby 30
Kellner, William 82
Kelly, Gene 93, 94, 94, 95
Kelly, Grace 101, 129
Kennedy, Edgar 44
Kennedy, George 166
Kes 184, 184
Kestrel Film Productions 184
Key Largo 95
Keystone Studios 18
Kid, The 22
Kid for Two Farthings, A 144
Kidd, Michael 148
Killing, The 148
Kim 38
Kind Hearts and Coronets 83, 83
King and I, The 144
King of Kings 16, 134
King Kong 40, 41
King in New York, A 86
Kiss Me Deadly 116, 117
Kiss of Death 88
Klondike 35
Klute 171, 171
Knack, The 152
Korda, Alexander 38, 50, 51, 82, 85
Korda, Zoltan 50
Krantz, Steve 172, 174
Krasker, Robert 74
Kubrick, Stanley 148, 150, 154, 155
Kurosawa, Akira 109

La Roque, Rod 16
Ladd, Alan 102, 103
Lady from Shanghai 85, 88, 89
Ladykillers, The 83, 108
Lahr, Bert 52, 53
Lancaster, Burt 101
Lanchester, Elsa 37, 38
Landlord, The 181
Lang, Charles 117
Lang, Fritz 117
Langdon, Harry 22, 23, 23, 46
Lansbury, Angela 148
Lardner, Ring Jr 166
Last Detail, The 176, 180, 181
Last Flight, The 27
Last Laugh, The 21, 27
Last Picture Show, The 176, 178, 179
Last Tango in Paris 179
Last Train from Gun Hill, The 125
Laughton, Charles 38
Laurel, Stan 46, 47
Laurie, Piper 148
Lavender Hill Mob, The 83
Lawford, Peter 135
Lawrence, Gertrude 144
Lawrence of Arabia 80, 134, 134
Lawson, Arthur 83, 106
Lawson, Wilfred 52
Leachman, Cloris 179
Lean, David 73, 74, 80, 81, 128, 134, 144
Lee, Christopher 108, 187
Legion of Decency 35
Leigh, Janet 148
Leigh, Vivien 56, 56, 57
Lemmon, Jack 67, 137
Lenny 7
Les Girls 112
Lester, Richard 150, 152, 187
Let's Make Love 112

Letter to Three Wives, A 98
Levin, Ira 158
Lewton, Val 71, 98
Lieberson, Sandy 184
Life and Death of Colonel Blimp, The 76
Lifeboat 129
Limelight 86
Listen to Britain 73
Little Caesar 32
Livesey, Roger 76
Lloyd, Harold 22, 23, 46
Loach, Ken 183, 184
Lodger, The 27
Lolita 148
Lombard, Carole 69
London Films 50, 51, 85, 106, 109
Loneliness of the Long-Distance Runner, The 141
Long Goodbye, The 166
Long Pants 23
Long Wait, The 38
Longest Day, The 134
Look Back in Anger 141
Lorre, Peter 117
Losey, Joseph 150, 152
Louis, Jean 119
Louisiana Story 50
Love Me Tonight 31, 31
Love Parade, The 27
Love Story 181, 181
Loy, Myrna 37, 41, 54
Lubitsch, Ernst 22, 27, 31, 54, 66, 69
Lugosi, Bela 108
Lumet, Sidney 150

M 117
M*A*S*H 166, 167
Macbeth 109, 158
MacArthur, Charles 66, 67
MacDonald, Jeanette 32, 59
MacDonald, Richard 152
MacGowran, Jack 152
MacGraw, Ali 181
MacKendrick, Sandy 108
MacLaine, Shirley 128, 136
Magnificent Ambersons, The 71
Mahler 184
Mainwaring, Daniel 119
Major Dundee 162
Malden, Karl 103
Male and Female 16
Maltese Falcon, The 78, 95
Mamoulian, Rouben 27, 31, 32, 134
Man from Laramie, The 122
Man in the White Suit, The 83, 108, 108
Man Who Knew Too Much, The 129
Man Who Shot Liberty Vallance, The 122
Manchurian Candidate, The 148, 148
Mandell, Daniel 77
Mankiewicz, Herman 71
Mankiewicz, Joseph 98, 103, 112, 134
Mann, Anthony 122
Mansfield, Jayne 112
March, Fredric 44, 77
Marie Walewska 54
Mark of Zorro, The 16
Marnie 130
Marriage Circle, The 22
Martin, Dean 125
Marvin, Lee 156, 166, 166
Marx Brothers, 27, 46
Marx, Groucho 47
Mary Poppins 143, 143
Mason, James 103, 112, 130, 144
Massey, Raymond 48, 51
Massine, Leonide 82, 106

Matter of Life and Death, A 76, 76
Matthau, Walter 67, 168
Matthews, Jessie 38, 39
Mayer, Carl 21
McAvoy, May 10
McCabe and Mrs Miller 158, 166
McCarey, Leo 46
McDowell, Malcolm 150, 151, 155
McDowell, Roddy 66
McLaglen, Victor 43, 106
McQueen, Steve 133, 148, 158, 158
Meat 160
Meeker, Ralph 117
Meet Me in St Louis 68, 68
Memorial Enterprises 150, 152
Men, The 103
Mercer, David 184
Meredith, Burgess 65
Merry Widow, The 20
Metro Pictures 24
Meyer, Emile 120
MGM 16, 20, 24, 30, 37, 46, 52, 54, 56, 59, 68, 93, 94, 98, 103, 120, 126, 130, 150, 154, 156, 166
Midnight Cowboy 156, 157
Midsummer Night's Dream, A 74
Milady's Revenge 187
Miles, Bernard 81
Miles, Sarah 152
Milestone, Lewis 30, 65, 67, 76
Milland, Ray 181
Miller, Arthur 137, 181
Miller, Jason 180
Mills, John 81
Minnelli, Liza 143, 146, 152
Minnelli, Vincente 67, 68, 98
Minnie and Moskovitz 161
Miracle of Morgan's Creek, The 68
Misfits, The 132, 137, 137
Mitchell, Margaret 56
Mitchum, Robert 76
Moana 50
Modern Times 46, 46
Modesty Blaise 138
Monkey Business 46
Monroe, Marilyn 90, 97, 98, 112, 114, 115, 115, 119, 132, 137
Monsieur Verdoux 86, 87
Montgomery, Robert 41
Moore, Robin 168
Morgan, Dennis 54
Morgan, Frank 52
Morgan, A Suitable Case for Treatment 141
Morley, Karen 36
Morocco 35
Morrissey, Paul 160
Mostel, Zero 97
Mr Deeds Goes to Town 41
Mr Smith Goes to Washington 41
Mrs Miniver 72
Mummy, The 109
Muni, Paul 41
Murnau, Friedrich 21, 50, 108
Music Lovers, The 184
Mutiny on the Bounty 134
Mutual Pictures 18
My Darling Clementine 8, 85, 85
My Fair Lady 52, 112, 142, 143
My Man Godfrey 37

Naked City 88
Naked Jungle, The 122
Nanook of the North 19, 19, 50

New Lot, The 74
Newman, Paul 135, 148, 163, 163
Newton, Robert 128, 144
Niblo, Fred 16
Nichols, Dudley 43
Nichols, Mike 176
Nicholson, Jack 158, 160, 180, 181
Night at the Opera, A 46, 47
Night Mail 80
Night Must Fall 141
Nine Lives of Fritz the Cat 174
Ninotchka 54
Niven, David 48, 66, 74, 74, 76, 76, 128
North by Northwest 129, 130, 131
North Sea 80
North Star, The 76
Nosferatu 108
Notorious 78, 78, 129, 130
Novarro, Ramon 10, 15, 16, 24

O Lucky Man 150
Oakland, Simon 130
Oates, Warren 162
Oberon, Merle 38, 66, 82
O'Brien, George 20, 21
O'Brien, Margaret 68
O'Brien, Willis 41
O'Casey, Sean 43
O'Connor, Donald 95
Odd Man Out 144
Of Mice and Men 64, 65
O'Flaherty, Liam 43
O'Hara, Maureen 66, 106
Oklahoma 144
Oland, Warner 35
Oliver 143, 144, 145
Oliver Twist 81, 144
Olivier, Sir Laurence 66, 73, 74, 75, 81, 104, 109, 111
On a Clear Day You can See Forever 146
On the Town 93, 93, 94
On the Waterfront 103, 105, 171
Ondra, Anny 27, 27
One A.M. 18
101 Dalmatians 172
O'Neal, Ryan 181
Orwell, George 104, 109
Osborne, John 138, 141
O'Toole, Peter 134, 134
Our Daily Bread 21, 24
Our Hospitality 23
Our Man Flint 138
Our Mother's House 141
Outlaw, The 86
Overlanders, The 80, 81

Pacino, Al 170
Paget, Debra 101
Pakula, Alan 171
Pal, George 122
Palance, Jack 97, 103
Pallette, Eugene 48
Palma, Carlo di 150
Pan, Hermes 43
Pangbourn, Franklin 69
Panic in the Streets 88, 96, 96
Paper Moon 179
Paramount 27, 30, 31, 32, 35, 46, 68, 72, 98, 103, 115, 122, 126, 129, 130, 150, 158, 170, 181
Passport to Pimlico 83
Pat Garrett and Billy the Kid 162
Pat and Mike 93
Pathé Pictures 24
Paths of Glory 148
Patton : Lust for Glory 166-7, 167
Pawnshop, The 18

Paxinou, Katina 72
Peace Game, The 154
Peck, Gregory 86
Peckinpah, Sam 162
Penn, Arthur 162
Pereira, Hal 122
Performance 184, 185
Perkins, Anthony 130
Peter Pan 61
Peters, Jean 119
Phantom of the Opera, The 109
Pickford, Mary 16
Pickup on South Street 118, 119
Picnic on the Grass 104
Pidgeon, Walter 120
Pinky 96
Pinocchio 61, 61
Pitts, ZaSu 20
Place in the Sun, A 103
Planet of the Apes 154, 154, 155
Platt, Louise 44
Play It Again, Sam 72
Pleasance, Donald 152
Plough and the Stars, The 43
Point Blank 156, 156, 158
Polanski, Roman 152, 156, 158, 180
Polglase, Van Nest 43
Pommer/UFA 27
Ponicsan, Darryl 180
Ponti, Carlo 150
Poor Cow 184
Pork Chop Hill 77
Porter, Edwin S. 12
Powell, Dick 98, 117
Powell, Michael 73, 76, 80, 82, 106
Powell, William 37, 54, 54, 117
Preminger, Inigo 166
Preminger, Otto 78, 79, 88, 117, 119, 135, 166
President's Analyst, The 154
Pressburger, Emeric 76, 82, 106
Price, Dennis 83
Price, Vincent 79, 126
Pride and Prejudice 74
Prima, Louis 172
Prisoner of Zenda, The (1922) 24
Prisoner of Zenda, The (1937) 48, 48
Private Life of Henry VIII, The 38, 38
Privilege 154
Psycho 129, 130, 130
Public Enemy 32, 33
Pumpkin Eater, The 141
Punishment Park 154
Purple Heart, The 76
Pygmalion 52, 52

Queen Kelly 20, 98
Queen of Spades, The 82, 82
Queen's Diamonds, The 187
Quiet Man, The 43, 104, 106, 106
Quinn, Anthony 38, 134
Quo Vadis 12

Rafferty, Chips 81, 81
Raft, George 41, 137
Raighton, Margo Ann 44
Rainer, Luise 54
Rains, Claude 48, 72, 134
Rank Films 141, 152, 187
Rathbone, Basil 48
Ray, Nicholas 119
Raye, Martha 86
Rear Window 129, 129
Rebecca 74, 78
Rebel without a Cause 91, 119, 119
Red River 80, 86, 87

188

Red Shoes, The 76, 82, 82, 106
Redford, Robert 163, 163
Redman, Joyce 138
Reed, Carol 73, 74, 80, 85, 144
Reed, Oliver 144, 187
Reisz, Karel 141
Remarque, Erich Maria 30
Rembrandt 38
Remick, Lee 117, 119
Remus Films 141
Renoir, Jean 32, 104
Repulsion 152
Rescued by Rover 12
Revenge of Frankenstein, The 109
Revillon Frères 19
Reynolds, Debbie 95
Richard III 109, 109, 111
Richardson, Ralph 51, 109, 135
Richardson, Tony 138, 141
Ring, The 27
Rio Bravo 125, 125
Riot in Cell Block 11 120
Rising of the Moon, The 43
Ritter, Thelma 119, 136
River, The 104, 104
R.K.O. Pictures 39, 41, 43, 52, 59, 61, 71, 78, 88
Roach, Hal 23, 46, 65
Robbins, Jerome 93, 148
Roberts, Rachel 141
Robin Hood 16, 48
Robinson, Edward G. 32, 41, 43, 97, 126, 136, 148
Robson, May 36, 44
Rodgers, Richard 31, 144
Roeg, Nicolas 183, 184
Rogers, Ginger 30, 38, 42, 43
Romeo and Juliet 52, 74
Room at the Top 140, 141
Rooney, Mickey 120
Rosa, Miklos 126
Rosemary's Baby 158, 158
Ross, Katharine 163, 176
Rossen, Robert 76, 86, 88, 148
Rosson, Harold 94
Rounseville, Robert 106
Rowlands, Gena 161
Ruddy, Francis 170
Rumann, Sig 46
Run of the Arrow 101
Russell, Harold 77, 77
Russell, Jane 90, 119
Russell, Ken 30, 183, 184
Russell, Rosalind 67
Ryan, Robert 162, 166
Ryan's Daughter 80

Saboteur 30
Sabu 50, 50
Safety Last 23, 23
Saint, Eve Marie 104, 130, 135
Salt, Waldo 156
Samson and Delilah 16, 98
San Francisco 37, 52, 58, 59
Sanda, Dominique 179
Sanders, George 98, 172
Sandrich, Mark 43
Sarris, Andrew 79
Saturday Night and Sunday Morning 141, 141
Savalas, Telly 166
Saville, Victor 38
Scaramouche 24
Scarface 39, 39, 41
Schaefer, Jack 103
Schaeffner, Franklin 155, 166
Scheider, Roy 168
Schlesinger, John 156
Schneider, Maria 179, 179
Schoedsack, Ernest 41
Schufftan, Eugene 148

Schulberg, Bud 103, 104
Schulman, Irving 119
Scott, George C. 119, 148, 167, 167
Segal, George 177
Seitz, John 24
Sellers, Peter 148
Selznick, David O. 39, 52, 56, 86, 98
Selznick International 44, 48, 56, 85
Sennett, Mack 18, 23
Sergeant York 72
Servant, The 152, 152
Seven Arts Productions 162
Seven Brides for Seven Brothers 148
Seven Days in May 148
Seven Year Itch, The 114, 115, 137
Shadows 160
Shane 102, 103, 124
Shanghai Express 34, 35
Shanghai Gesture, The 35
Sharaff, Irene 68
Sharif, Omar 134, 134, 146
She Done Him Wrong 35
She Wore a Yellow Ribbon 85
Shearer, Moira 82, 106
Shepherd, Cybill 178, 179
Sheriff, Paul 74
Sherman, Richard and Robert 142
Sherriff, R. C. 37
Sherwood, Robert 77
Shingleton, Wilfred 81
Shoulder Arms 18, 24
Siegel, Don 119, 120, 168
Sign of the Cross, The 16
Signoret, Simone 141
Silk Stockings 115
Simmons, Jean 81
Sinatra, Frank 128, 148
Singin' in the Rain 94, 94, 96
Siodmak, Robert 88
Sleeper 154
Smith, C. Aubrey 31, 48
Snow White and the Seven Dwarfs 52, 59, 59, 60, 61
Some Like It Hot 136, 137
Something's Got to Give 137
Sound of Music, The 144, 144
South Pacific 144
South Riding 38
Southerner, The 104
Spartacus 134
Spector, Phil 160
Spiegel, Sam 128, 134
Spillane, Mickey 38, 117
Squaw Man, The 16
Stagecoach 44, 44, 85
Stalag 17 128
Stander, Lionel 44, 152
Star 144
Star is Born, A 44, 45, 112
Stark, Richard 156
Steamboat Bill Jr 23
Steiger, Rod 101, 103
Sternberg, Joseph von 27, 30, 35, 39
Stevens, George 101, 103
Stewart, Donald Ogden 48
Stewart, James 88, 101, 117, 122, 129
Sting, The 163
Stoker, Bram 108
Story of Dr Wassall, The 72
Story of G.I. Joe, The 76
Stothart, Herbert 52
Stranger, The 85, 88
Strangers on a Train 129
Strategic Air Command 122
Streetcar Named Desire, A 103

Streisand, Barbra 143, 144, 146, 146
Stroheim, Erich von 19, 19, 20, 98
Strong Man, The 23
Sturges, Preston 67, 68, 69
Sullivan, Barry 98
Summertime 80
Sunrise 21, 21
Sunset Boulevard 94, 96, 98, 99
Super Panavision 134
Surtees, Robert 126
Sutherland, Donald 166, 171
Swamp Water 104
Swanson, Gloria 16, 20, 94, 98
Sweet Charity 146
Sweet Smell of Success, The 108
Sword in the Stone, The 172
Sydney, Sylvia 31

Tabu 21, 50
Tales of Hoffman, The 76, 106, 107
Tamiroff, Akim 72
Target for Tonight 80
Tashlin, Frank 112
Taste of Honey, A 141
Taylor, Elizabeth 6, 103, 134, 135, 177
Taylor, Robert 28, 54
Taylor, Robert (director) 174
Taza, Son of Cochise 101
Tcherina, Ludmilla 83, 106
Technicolor 44, 52, 82, 103, 106, 115
Tempest, The 120
Ten Commandments, The (1924) 16
Ten Commandments, The (1956) 126, 127
Ten Seconds to Hell 166
Tevis, Walter 148
Thalberg, Irving 24
That's Entertainment 54
Thesiger, Ernest 37
They Were Expendable 76
They Who Dare 77
Thief of Bagdad, The (1925) 14, 16, 51
Thief of Bagdad, The (1940) 50
Thieves' Highway 88
Thin Man, The 36, 37, 54, 59
Things to Come 51, 51
Third Man, The 84, 85
13, Rue Madeleine 88
Thirty-Nine Steps, The 50, 50, 130
This Happy Breed 74
This Sporting Life 141, 141, 150
Three Musketeers, The (1921) 16
Three Musketeers, The (1973) 186, 187, 187
3 : 10 to Yuma 124, 125
Throne of Blood 109
THX 1138 154
Tidyman, Ernest 168
Tierney, Gene 79
To Be or Not to Be 68-9, 69
To Catch a Thief 129
To Have and Have Not 79
Todd, Mike 128
Toland, Gregg 65, 66, 77
Tom Jones 138, 138
Too Late the Hero 166
Top Hat 43
Tora! Tora! Tora! 166
Touch of Evil 88
Tourneur, Jacques 71
Tracy, Spencer 32, 59, 93,

117
Tramp, Tramp, Tramp 23
Trash 160
Trauner, Alexander 137
Travers, P. L. 143
Treasure of Sierra Madre, The 95
Trevor, Claire 44, 44
Trintignant, Jean-Louis 179
Trouble with Harry, The 129
Twelve Angry Men 119
Twentieth Century Fox see Fox
Two Cities Films 74
Two-Faced Woman 54
2001 : A Space Odyssey 120, 154, 154, 155, 160

Underworld 39
Underworld USA 119
United Artists 16, 22, 23, 39, 44, 46, 48, 69, 86, 95, 101, 105, 117, 119, 128, 135, 137, 138, 148, 152, 156, 172, 179, 183, 184
Universal Pictures 30, 37, 48, 108, 122
Ustinov, Peter 74

Vagabond, The 18
Valentino, Rudolph 24
Van Dyke, W. S. 37, 59
Variety 27
Veidt, Conrad 72
Vertigo 129
Vidor, King 24, 85, 86
Vigo, Jean 150
VistaVision 109, 115, 126
Viva Villa! 86
Viva Zapata 103, 119
Voight, Jon 156, 157

Wagonmaster 85
Walbrook, Anton 82
Walk in the Sun, A 76, 77
Walkabout 184
Wallach, Eli 137
Walsh, George 16
Walsh, Raoul 16
Wanger, Walter 39, 44
War and Peace 24
War of the Worlds, The 122, 122
Warhol, Andy 160, 160
Warner Bros 27, 30, 31, 32, 48, 72, 79, 88, 112, 119, 122, 125, 143, 155, 158, 162, 171, 180, 184
Warner, H. B. 98
Warner, Jack 143
Warner-Pathé 152
Warren, Robert Penn 88
Watkins, Peter 154
Watt, Harry 80, 81
Way Ahead, The 74, 74
Way to the Stars, The 52
Wayne, John 44, 44, 86, 106, 122, 125
Webb, Clifton 79

Wedding March, The 20
Welch, Raquel 187
Welles, Orson 67, 71, 85, 86, 88
Wellman, William 27, 32, 44
Wells, H. G. 50, 51, 122
West, Mae 35, 35, 46
West Side Story 148, 149
Wexler, Haskell 177
Whale, James 37
What? 158
What Price Glory? 16
What's Up Doc? 179
Where the Sidewalk Ends 79, 88
Whirlpool 79, 88
Whisky Galore 83, 108
Whitelaw, Billie 152
Whole Town's Talking, The 43
Who's Afraid of Virginia Woolf? 176-7, 177
Widmark, Richard 97, 119
Wild Bunch, The 162
Wild in the Streets 154
Wild One, The 119
Wilde, Brandon de 103
Wilder, Billy 67, 78, 98, 115, 137
Wilson, Dooley 72
Winchester 73 122
Wings 26, 27, 32
Winnie the Pooh and the Honey Tree 172
Wise, Robert 148
Wiseman, Joseph 138
Wizard of Oz, The 52, 53
Woman of Paris, The 22
Woman on the Beach, The 104
Women, The 37
Women in Love 182, 183, 183
Woodfall Films 138, 141
Woods, Eddie 32
Wray, Fay 41
Wrong Man, The 129
Wuthering Heights 65, 66, 67, 74
Wyler, William 66, 77, 126, 144

Yates, Peter 156
Yellow Submarine, The 172, 173, 174
York, Michael 187
York, Susannah 138
You Can't Take it with You 41
You Only Live Once 117
Young, Freddie 134
Young, Terence 138
Young, Victor 128
Young Mr Lincoln 85

Zanuck, Darryl 65, 66, 88, 112
Zero de Conduite 150
Zinnemann, Fred 101, 103
Zsigmond, Vilmos 158

Most of the illustrations in the book come from the personal collection of the author.
The publishers and author would like to thank Kevin Gough-Yates for his advice and encouragement in the preparation of this book. Special thanks too to Julian Fox and to the following individuals and film companies for the use of visual material:
Kevin Brownlow; Martin Heath; Peter Howden; Colin Payne; Eric Sargeant; Don Woolland.
Charles Berman, United Artists; John Halas, Halas and Batchelor Cartoon Films Ltd; Barbara de Lord, Fox-Rank; K. F. Matthews, Rank Film Distributors; Mike Munn, Columbia-Warner; Stills Department, National Film Archive; Mike Tither, Walt Disney.
Cinema International Corporation/MGM, Paramount, Universal; Embassy Films; EMI; Hammer Films; London Films.